A Second Opinion

Theories and Observations on Life and Human Behavior

By:
Emily Maroutian

A Second Opinion

Theories and Observations on Life
and Human Behavior

by:
Emily Maroutian

Author photo by Freddie Mendoza
Double Arrow Cover Image © JUPITERIMAGES

ISBN: 1-4404-5232-6
ISBN-13: 978-1-4404-5232-1

Second Printing

Printed and bound in the United States of America by Createspace, a division of Amazon.com

Los Angeles, California

This book is dedicated to YOU.
May you find peace amidst the chaos of your mind.

Acknowledgements:

Many individuals have helped me grow emotionally, mentally and spiritually. There are far too many to list.

This book is in gratitude to those who have taught me about life and have helped me understand myself better. Thank you for all the lessons you have taught me directly and indirectly, knowingly and unknowingly.

Acknowledgement must be given to my loving mother who has always given her all and my animated sisters (there is never a dull moment with the two of you.)

I would also like to acknowledge the great philosopher Alan Watts and His Holiness the Dalai Lama for pointing me to the road to compassion and enlightenment.

A special thanks to LaGina Phillips for her copyediting services and Freddie Mendoza for the author photo.

Author's Note:

This book holds observations and theories collected over years of personal experiences and studying philosophy.

Most of the information provided in this book is not original or new. In fact, some of the information has been around for thousands of years.

The chapters were created as levels, specifically arranged for the best possible understanding of all concepts presented. Each chapter is only a fraction of the discussion available on each topic and meant as introductions to the ideas presented therein.

I do not claim to be an expert on psychology, human behavior or sociology. I am merely an observer.

For this reason, I have purposely chosen to omit page numbers and chapter numbers from this book.

We, as a society, become caught up in measuring progress. We watch the clock, not enjoying what we do. We count calories, not enjoying what we eat. We count miles, not enjoying the journey.

Read, not for accomplishment but for enjoyment. Don't become caught up on progress, just do it. You will finish when you finish.

Introduction:

Most self-help books will give you a long list of things to do to change yourself into a better person.

Unfortunately, this concept makes the assumption that if it worked for the author, it will work for others as well. It also assumes that the author knows what would make *you* a better person.

No one can know your thoughts, feelings, beliefs, hopes, dreams, memories or experiences. No one else can know you or the world you live in the way you do. The only person who has that kind of access is you.

In this book, there is but one intention: awareness. When you are aware of your thoughts, feelings, beliefs and behaviors, you have the power of choice. You can then decide what works in your life and what does not.

We have been preprogrammed from birth with beliefs, thoughts and behaviors that we have formed into habits.

Habits get in the way of awareness because they force us to live our lives asleep in routine. If we always do what we have always done, we will always get what we have always gotten. Without awareness, we react to life based on how we usually react to life.

I'm not offering to make you a better person. I'm offering you the power of choice through awareness and the freedom to choose without the influence of someone else's actions, behaviors and habits.

This book offers a tool to guide you in dumping the thoughts, feelings and habits that hinder awareness and cause suffering.

Through awareness, you can shatter illusions and false beliefs, reveal myths and truths and understand what makes you happy and gives your life meaning.

You are then free to be you and not someone else's idea of a better you.

Ultimately, it is your decision what you choose for your life and yourself. My only goal is to offer you a cleaner filter to see your life and decisions through.

This book is my gift to you. It is a collection of philosophies, theories and observations that I believe will alter your sense of self and the world around you.

"The World of Beliefs"

"The mind is its own place, and in itself, can make Heaven of Hell, and a Hell of Heaven." -John Milton, Paradise Lost

When I was a child, I was always fascinated with other people's beliefs. Why is it that we all live in the same world and yet live worlds apart? How could so many people believe so many contradicting things?

I experienced many internal conflicts with the ideas of right and wrong. One person's right was another person's wrong. A wrong in one situation was right in another. It seemed like nothing was consistent and everything was very contradictory.

As I grew older and delved deeper into philosophy, I realized that there were far more questions than there were answers.

While I can't offer any perfect answers, I can offer my views, opinions, thoughts and ideas about these important questions. It is another perspective to consider, a different opinion to reflect on.

Our beliefs are an important aspect of our lives. In fact, they are so important that I'm willing to go so far as to say that they shape our experiences.

Most people believe that experiences shape our beliefs, but I believe that it is our beliefs that shape our experiences.

We all carry around harmful beliefs disguised as facts. Some beliefs are about the self; I'm stupid, unworthy, sick, unlucky, I'll never be happy, rich or pretty. Other beliefs are about groups of people; other societies, cultures, religions, sexes, races, etc.

Our beliefs are reinforced by our actions, behaviors and feelings. How can we know if they are true? How can we test our beliefs against reality when we view reality through our beliefs?

If we are in pain, it is because of a belief that does not coincide with reality.

Our beliefs are so commonly held and so deeply believed that we don't even realize that they are just things that we, at some point in our lives, decided to believe as facts.

We have a powerful and unknowing ability to make ourselves think that beliefs are facts. We fight for them, suffer for them and die for them.

We carry around beliefs about our families, our friends, groups of people, society and even ourselves.

Many things we see and experience in our everyday lives support our beliefs. Whether our beliefs are legitimate or false, we can always find evidence to strengthen them. This is why so many different people can hold such different and sometimes contradicting beliefs.

Not only do we need to question what we believe and why we believe it, but we must also look at why false beliefs can appear real.

The mind is selective in what it chooses to remember. So why does one mind choose to remember one thing while another mind remembers another?

Two people witnessing the same event can remember and experience different things. How is it that their minds remember and take in information differently?

Our court system does not accept eyewitness testimony as substantial evidence because they know that the information differs with each eyewitness even though they all witnessed the same event.

I once read that the mind only understands 30 percent of what it experiences a day and remembers only 10 percent of what it understood.

If you only remember such a small percentage of what you understood in any given day, it is very likely that your mind is selective about what it wants to remember.

So what would be important enough for your mind to absorb and what would be considered useless information that won't even register in the mind? Our beliefs determine the information the mind chooses to remember.

We each contain a filter within our minds. It sorts through the millions of bits of information we receive everyday and only pays attention to that which is consistent with our beliefs.

Everyone interprets information through his or her filter. Because of this reason, no one receives the full picture or the full experience. We can only have partial knowledge.

The information you receive is perceived in relation to what you believe and who you are at that given moment in time.

For instance, if I say the word apple and ask a random group of people to tell me the first thing that comes to their mind, I will get several different responses.

If you just bought an Apple computer or an Apple iPod, you might think of the company or its products.

If you are a teacher, it might remind you of the first day of school when your students bring you apples as a sign of respect.

If you study Christianity, you might think of the Adam and Eve story with the apple and think of the apple representing temptation.

If you are hungry at this moment, you might think of a big juicy red apple you wish you could eat. You might think of the apple tea you drank, or the applesauce you just fed your toddler.

However, the information will change for you at a different period. If I asked you tomorrow, you might have a different answer.

Think of a movie you watched as a child. Can you remember how different it seemed when you re-watched it years later? You saw scenes you didn't remember before. You understood things that you didn't understand then. It's almost as if you are watching the movie with different eyes.

The same thing happens with books and music. The book does not change and yet every time you read it, you discover new things.

The thing didn't change, how you relate to it changes. How you feel changes. Who you are is a different person with a different filter therefore you interpret it differently.

The interpretation is very rarely an accurate one since we cannot experience something new without comparing it to something we have experienced before.

The Blind Men and the Elephant

A group of blind men went to the zoo and visited an elephant. One blind man touched its side and said, "The elephant is like a wall." The next blind man touched its trunk and said, "The elephant is like a snake." The next blind man touched its leg and said, "The elephant is like a column." The last blind man touched its tail and said, "The elephant is like a broom." Then the four blind men started to fight, each one believing that his opinion was the right one. Each only understood the part he had touched; none of them understood the whole.

We all create distinctions in the mind. This is due to partial knowledge. All knowledge we possess is partial knowledge. Like the pieces of the elephant, we can only know one thing at a time.

Let's say you walk over to another part of the elephant and touch its leg. So now, you know that the tail is like a broom and the leg is like a column.

Even though you have gained more knowledge, it is still partial knowledge.

Now that we've decided that the elephant is a column with a broom, we face even more questions.

Is the broom first and the column second? Is the broom hanging from the column? Is the broom there to sweep dirt off the column? Is the column protecting the broom? Is the broom more important than the column?

Each additional piece of new information comes with more questions that need answers in order for us to understand.

You might be able to say, "I see the elephant, I'm not blind. It's big and grey." However, big and grey are just distinctions within our minds.

You don't "see" the elephant. You see distinctions from your mind and past experiences. Just as when you look at others and you say, "I see John, he's mean and rude." You don't see John. You only see your own judgment of the distinctions.

Is any of it true? Can you really know the elephant without comparing it to something you've already experienced?

If you couldn't use experiences you already had to describe the elephant, how would you describe it?

If you describe parts of it, you will describe it based on things you know, like the column and the broom. If you describe it as a whole and say it is big and grey, you are still using distinctions from previous experiences. You have seen and experienced both big and grey and that is why you can describe it. Are they still true?

The elephant is big. If the elephant were standing next to a skyscraper, would you still describe the elephant as big? Perhaps. However, why is it big?

It's only big in relation to you. In relation to the skyscraper, it's very small. Therefore, you are still using yourself and your experiences to describe the elephant.

Is the same true for the elephant? If the elephant cannot see color and only sees grey, then to him, everything is grey therefore nothing is grey. The elephant does not know the distinction of grey because all he sees is grey.

The elephant may not feel big either. In relation to all the other elephants, he may feel normal.

This is where the problem lies. We can't experience something new without first comparing it to something we've already experienced.

When we meet someone new, our minds search for and isolate distinctions that we recognize in others we have known.

For some women it seems like they date the same man repeatedly but in different bodies. Are they really the same man?

Even though it is a new person with different memories and experiences, we immediately separate, label and judge. We react to them as if they are another person.

Much like the parts of the elephant, we can't see the whole. Most of the time, we don't want to see the whole. It is far easier to compare people to others we have known and move on.

We see distinctions in others because it makes it easier for us to understand them.

We hold beliefs about distinctions and when we recognize those distinctions in others, it triggers our beliefs. For example, say I watch a black man rob a liquor store and I now believe that all black men are criminals. If I come across another black man, I will judge him, not for his own actions, but for the actions of the criminal black man. He no longer has his own identity. He now holds distinctions that are negative for me.

The filter, that narrows in on distinctions, also fuels discrimination and hate. We only see the bad or negative in others. It is what we choose to see because it is what we believe to be true. The filter reinforces false beliefs and gives them strength.

Can you think of a belief you may have about a group of people? Is it true? Can ALL members of any group be the same? If a group of people hold one similar distinction, does it make them all the same?

Our brains are designed to view one point at a time. When you look at a picture, your eyes can't look at the whole picture. They scan the picture and your brain puts it together.

We can't think two thoughts at the same time, we can't say two words at the same time and we can't look at two points at the same time.

Have you looked at a painting and noticed something you hadn't seen before? It's very likely that your eyes had not scanned to that area of the picture.

Our minds can only focus on one thing at a time; this is like the blind men and the elephant. Imagine if you touch the right leg of the elephant and then I switched the elephant with another one without your knowledge. Then you touched the right leg of that elephant. Would you know that you touched two different elephants?

The experience feels the same for you, but not for the elephant. It is a different elephant. It may be an abused elephant that becomes violent when it is touched.

The first elephant may have felt nothing when it was touched, but the second may be experiencing extreme emotions from the touch. Even though the touch felt the same for you, it was not the same touch.

We cannot experience the whole elephant all at once. We can only experience pieces at a time that we can compare to experiences from our past. However, experiences from our past can hold information that does not fit into the current situation.

Our minds are designed to fill in the blank when information is missing. We have to work consciously to look at things as they are, without labels, judgment or comparison to the past.

Imagine for a moment that a man dressed in all black; black shoes, black pants, black jacket, and a black ski mask is walking down a deserted alley with no lights. A black car with no headlights is approaching the man but stops before he hits him. How did the driver see the man?

Try to imagine the story you just read in your mind. Read it again several times if you must and imagine it in your mind. Can you figure out how the driver saw the man?

The answer is far easier than you think. Many people I know came up with numerous intricate responses as to why the driver stopped. Some said that there was another car approaching from the other side with their headlights on. Others believed that it was the man's shoes reflecting the moonlight and one person said it was the light from the moon and stars.

It's very simple. It was day. Nowhere in the story did it say it was night. Did your mind imagine the story at night?

Our minds automatically visualize the story at night. The man is wearing a ski mask, which we associate with criminal activity that usually takes place at night. He's walking down an alley, which we associate with dark and scary because people usually get attacked in alleys and that reinforces the criminal image.

The mind automatically fills in the night because of all of these factors and information from the past.

We must be conscious of how we judge others because by hearing one piece of information about someone, our minds may fill in the rest with false information from *our* past that is not in relation to that person.

All of these factors were set in place for our ancestors to help in their survival. You only need to see a leopard once to know that you need to run for your life. You would not walk up to one thinking that maybe this one is different.

However, our natural design works against us in society. It works well in nature but not in civilization. You only need to see one poisonous cobra to know that all cobras are poisonous.

There are certain true statements that we can make about the human race as a whole but none about specific groups within humanity.

Most of the statements are social distinctions that we learn from our parents, friends, TV, teachers or others. They are not facts; our beliefs make them true in our experience.

We are not separated by color, race, religion, etc. Our minds are designed to separate, label and judge to make things easier for us to understand.

The world itself is whole. We divide parts of the world and label them in order for us to understand it better. Our mind is a separator. Nevertheless, that doesn't mean that the world is separate.

If I placed a picture on graph paper with little boxes that divide parts of the picture, does that mean the picture is not whole?

Beginning artists sometimes use this paper to help them learn how to draw. Drawing parts of the whole is far easier than trying to draw the whole all at once. We must divide to see and understand. Unfortunately, we have done it for so long and we do it so often that we forget that we were the ones that separated things.

We separate planets, stars, black holes, etc, in order to understand them. Does that mean that they are not a part of the universe as a whole?

We separate organs from the body in order to understand how the body works better. Does that mean the organs are separate from the body?

We see things in the world as separate. We see a tree, a river, a plant, etc. However, these things are not separate things.

The tree exists in relation to the sun, water and the environment in which it grows. It is not separate from any of those things.

Everything in the world is related to each other. One thing consists of another. Nothing is individual and separate; we perceive them as such.

The Earth itself would not exist without its precise location and distance from the sun. The sun would not exist without the universe or space.

Our minds create separation, distinction and division. Then we take what we have separated and judge it based on our previous experiences. After we judge it, we label it and put it away in our minds to use later when we come across something similar.

All of our lives, we have been gathering information to make our lives easier. Unfortunately, this has created an even bigger problem for us. Instead of making our lives easier, it fuels hate, violence, injustice and war, thus making things far worse.

Our filter, aside from sorting out information that reinforces our false beliefs, receives the same information as someone else might receive but interprets it differently.

Imagine if you placed red-tinted glasses on when you were a child and it made everything you saw red. Then, as you got older, you forgot that you had the glasses on. Everything was red to you but you no longer saw the red because everything was red.

That is your filter. You can change the color of your glasses but you can't take them off.

It's not a matter of getting rid of your filter or taking off your glasses, it's about being aware that you have them.

If you keep in mind that you view things differently from others, it will make communication and understanding easier. Just like when we realize that our beliefs are just that: beliefs.

Because we all have different filters or glasses on, we all hold different beliefs, opinions and truths. This can cause many problems in relationships, communication and diplomacy. However, it can have an even more powerful affect on how we view ourselves.

There are beliefs about ourselves that we all carry around that are not true.

Some people believe that they are stupid when in fact they are intelligent. Some time ago, they decided that they were stupid and their filter changed.

They now filter out intelligent decisions and only focus on the events, actions or conversations that make them feel stupid. It reinforces their belief that they are stupid.

We all do stupid things sometimes but to someone who believes that they are stupid, it's devastating. They go through life holding themselves back because of this belief. Failing at a task also reinforces that belief. We all fail, but we are only failures if we accept failure as our destiny.

We all hold limiting beliefs about ourselves. Some blame their limitations on their sex, culture, skin color, genes, body type, etc.

"The World of Beliefs"

There is a famous story about fleas that are placed in a jam jar. The fleas jump to the top of the jar and hit their heads on the roof of the jar. Eventually, the fleas learn to jump high enough where they don't hit their heads on the roof of the jar.

When the fleas are taken out of the jar, even though they hold the ability to jump eight to ten inches high, they only jump as high as the jam jar.

Zoo trainers train elephants in a similar way. When the elephant is young, they tie the leg of the elephant with rope. The elephant tries to move around and can only go so far before it is tugged back. Then when the elephant is grown, even though it is strong enough to break the rope, it doesn't even try because it has been conditioned to believe that it can't.

Humans have also been conditioned to believe that they are far more limited than they actually are. Some of this conditioning comes from the parents. Some parents pass on their own limitations to their children without even realizing it.

Some of the conditioning comes from society and some of it comes from the person themselves. Either way, we all have beliefs about what we are capable of doing that aren't true.

Barack Obama did not grow up believing that there were only a minimal amount of things he could accomplish in his life just because he was black. There were tens of thousands, if not millions, of children growing up in America at the same time, believing that they could never be president because they are black. Therefore, they never tried.

We don't always receive empowerment from our parents, teachers, friends or family. We must empower ourselves. We are responsible for ourselves; we are responsible for our beliefs, thoughts, feelings and actions. We may not have been when we were children, but we are no longer children.

When our beliefs change, our filter changes as well. Soon enough our thoughts change, our feelings change, our actions change and the world changes. The world changes because we change.

Someone once told me that the world is a mirror of the self. If you are feeling angry, you will encounter people and things that make you feel angry. If you are happy, you will encounter people and things that make you feel happy. I believe this is due to our filters.

Siblings living in the same home can grow up having completely different views of the world. Some people might see the world as a cold and selfish place while other people might see the world as a place for creation and hope.

Each person acts accordingly to their belief of the world and receives feedback through the filter that reinforces their beliefs. Those who see the world as a cold and selfish place only see that. They react coldly, choosing to do things that only benefit themselves. Then when others react to their actions coldly, it reinforces their belief that the world is a cold place.

Which person's view is the correct one? All views of the world are correct if we believe them. We already understand the power of beliefs and how they can alter the way we see things.

Two people performing the same task can view the task in different ways. Imagine if you walked up to two men chipping away at a rock. You ask the first man, "What are you doing?" He answers, "Oh I'm just chipping away at this rock." Then you ask the second man the same question. He answers, "I'm building a cathedral."

What is the difference between the two men? They are both performing the same exact act, chipping at a rock. Yet one is just performing a job and the other is filled with purpose and peace.

The first man might choose to quit that job believing it's a waste of his time and even feel resentment toward it. The second man might choose to dedicate his entire life to building because it gives him a sense of purpose.

How we choose to view our environment, our family, society, life, the world and ourselves makes a dramatic difference in who we are, how we feel and what we choose to do.

The world acts as a mirror because of our filter. Whatever emotion or deed you choose to project on to the world will be mirrored back. It's not magic, it's psychology. If I believe that the world is full of angry people, my mind will pay more attention to people who are angry. Moreover, once I see an angry person, it will confirm my belief.

If we look for the bad in others, we will find the bad. What we seek, we will find. A pickpocket will not see the saint, only his pockets.

Therefore, a corrupt person views the world as corrupt so he can justify being corrupt.

If he viewed the world and his victims as just, honest, loving and caring people, he could not bring himself to act as such.

Therefore, he views the world as a cold, selfish place full of people who stand in the way of his happiness or way of life.

Any act can be justified in the mind regardless of the savagery. Even if the person sees the act as retaliation for the same cruel act that was committed on him.

However, if we saw each other and the world from a more inclusive perspective, we could never bring ourselves to commit crimes against each other. We couldn't justify it because the perspective would leave no room for justification.

The House of 1,000 Mirrors

In a small far-away village, there was a place known as The House of 1,000 Mirrors.

A small, happy dog decided to visit. When he arrived, he bounced happily up the stairs to the doorway of the house. He looked through the doorway with his ears lifted high and his tail wagging as fast as it could.

To his great surprise, he found himself staring at 1,000 other happy little dogs with their tails wagging just as fast as his. He smiled and was answered with 1,000 great smiles just as warm and friendly. As he left the House, he thought to himself, "This is a wonderful place. I will come back and visit it often."

In this same village, an angry, little dog decided to visit the same house. He climbed the stairs and anxiously hung his head low as he looked into the door. When he saw the 1,000 unfriendly looking dogs staring back at him, he growled at them out of fear and was horrified to see 1,000 little dogs growling back at him. He ran off thinking, "What a horrible place. I will never go back there again."

QUOTE:

"We lie loudest when we lie to ourselves." -Eric Hoffer, *The Passionate State Of Mind, and Other Aphorisms*

"The World of Myths"

"The great enemy of the truth is very often not the lie - deliberate, contrived and dishonest - but the myth - persistent, persuasive and unrealistic."
-John F. Kennedy

The difference between the world of beliefs and the world of myths is that myths are believed by a larger group of people and often continue to exist regardless of whether we do.

Our personal beliefs either die with us or are passed on to the people around us; myths continue on a societal level.

There are some common myths that are shared by most societies and then there are myths held specifically to each culture.

Let's look at some commonly held myths ...

The Myth of Independence:

Independence is a myth. There is no such thing as an independent person. We are all dependent on each other.

Our whole culture is designed to make you believe that you can have independence if you just purchased a specific car, attended a specific college or worked at a specific job.

If we looked at the history of the shirt you're wearing as a simple example, we would see that independence in our current way of life is impossible.

Your shirt was once just cotton. People in a field somewhere planted cotton plants, watered them, and picked them. Then it was transported on a truck or airplane to a factory where hundreds of others worked to put your shirt together. They dyed it, designed it, cut it and sewed it together.

Then it was transported, again by plane or truck, to stores where sales people sold you the shirt.

We must also factor in the advertising agencies who worked hard to make you familiar with the brand. The truck and airplane builders it was transported with, the road it was transported on and the millions of other factors that had to be put in place in order for you to be able to buy that shirt. You can see that your shirt alone was the product of hundreds or maybe thousands of people working together.

Now imagine the food you eat, the car you drive, the road you drive it on, the house you live in, the furniture, etc.

You are dependent on others to provide for you. Independence is a myth. In fact, your whole existence was dependent on two people finding each other. We can't forget about the doctors, nurses, teachers, babysitters, family, friends, neighbors and all the other people who have contributed to your life.

Your whole life has been dependent on others. Your education is especially dependent on others. If you consider yourself even remotely intelligent, it is due to your parents, family, friends, teachers, strangers, TV, movies, books and thousands of others in your lifetime who have contributed to your knowledge.

We can't forget the millions of other people who have existed before you, who have invented, created, and searched for the knowledge you currently possess.

If you have ever had the experience of lying in a hospital bed awaiting surgery, as I have, that is the moment when you can truly feel how dependent you are on others. Your life is in the hands of doctors, nurses, anesthesiologists and machines that pump fluids and medicine and that measure important vital functions.

From the most important to the trivial, we are dependent on others. Even when we can't see them, even though we don't know them.

If we can realize that we are in fact dependent on others, even though we can't see them, perhaps we can narrow the divide we feel toward others.

People you don't know contribute to your life. You are surrounded by things that were made by people you have never met. You know information collected by people you have never met.

Your whole life works because others exist; police, firefighters, educators, telephone operators, sales people, pilots, receptionists, writers, etc.

There is a whole world of people whose existence makes your life easier. They are mothers, fathers, brothers, sisters, black, white, brown, female, male, gay, straight, Christian, Muslim, Jewish, fat, skinny, tall, short, any distinction that your mind can come up with, aids in your existence.

Everything you love or enjoy from life is because of someone else. How can you possibly be independent?

The Myth of Security:

There is a common misconception that if we just repeat the same things over and over again, we will have stability and therefore feel secure in our lives.

We believe we have stability and security if we stay at the same job for a certain period, if we have been married for a certain amount of years, have purchased a house or received a diploma.

These are also false beliefs that we carry around that cause us suffering.

Security is a myth. There are false senses of security but never real security. We like to think that if we lived in an insecure environment then we would be plagued with anxiety and fear all the time. Yet, people with "secure" jobs and houses are the ones who are the most anxious because they are afraid of losing them.

A recent study on the happiest countries revealed that the happiest residences weren't necessarily residing in wealthy countries. In fact, the countries that offered the most opportunities for wealth had more unhappy citizens than happy ones.

We stay in jobs and relationships we are miserable in because it feeds our false sense of security. We fear change because it reminds us that stability is a myth.

Change is constant. Change is life. Your body goes through changes every day, the weather changes every day; your environment is always changing.

The Earth is constantly changing. One day we might have an earthquake, tsunami, hurricanes, fires, floods, accidents, etc.

We sit on a giant rock that is rotating around a big ball of fire, in an ever-expanding universe so large that our minds can't even conceive of the measurement. Can we really expect to have security because we have a nice, gated house? Or is it because we sit in a car and drive to work every day, repeating the same things over and over again?

Just because we have found routine or created habits doesn't mean we have security. In fact, it just makes us blind to the change constantly happening all around us.

Life is change. Without change, there would be no life. Music is only music because of the changes of the notes. If we held one note for a long period it wouldn't be music, it would be noise. It is because the notes change that it becomes music.

In fact, the only thing you can count on is change.

The Myth of Ownership and Possession:

If I asked you the question, "What do you own?" what would your answer be? Would you list a house, car, cell phone or clothes? Do you own these things?

What does it mean to own something? Ultimately, anything you might own belongs to nature. You, too, are a part of nature. Can nature own itself?

If we break everything down on a quantum level then everything is matter, energy and/or space. Nothing in the universe owns anything.

Does the sun own trees? Do trees own birds?

You liver cannot survive in your body without your heart, does that mean that your heart owns your liver? Does your brain own your kidneys? If your kidneys were to fail without your brain's permission, would your brain continue to survive?

There may be things that exist because you created them or purchased them, but no one can really own anything. You don't even own your body.

In fact, if it weren't for the sun, earth, water, animals and vegetation, you wouldn't be here, so does that mean nature owns you?

Once it is time, your body will go into the ground. In the ground, it will dissolve into the dirt. The dirt will house and feed plants. Animals will eat the plants, other animals will eat those animals and back it all goes to nature.

We forget that even the gadgets we purchase in the stores come from nature. All elements, material and parts originate from nature.

Even the land we are born on is not ours. I hear people talk about their property and their land. Just because we have been born into a land that we have named, such as the United States of America, Italy or France, doesn't mean that it belongs to us or those who currently live on it.

How can we own a part of nature? What is it that makes us believe we own it? Is it the piece of paper approved by government? Is it because we traded little colored paper we call money for a government-approved paper that states we own something?

Land is nature also. There is no U.S., Italy, Russia or France, only Earth. There is no Mars, Venus, Jupiter or Earth, only galaxies. There is no sun, moon, black hole or galaxies, only the universe.

We have created the distinctions of these things in our minds so that we can separate, label and map. This helps our minds understand and remember. Unfortunately, we have forgotten that we created these distinctions and believe them to be truths.

We cannot own any part of nature, just as we cannot own any part of our bodies. This is also a false sense of security and can cause anxiety.

If you own something, then that means you can lose it. The thoughts, feelings and worries can become a prison for someone who "owns" many things. "What if I lose it?"

Ultimately, if you don't want to lose anything all you have to do is realize that you don't own anything. You can't lose anything if you never owned anything.

Nature doesn't struggle to own, possess or control. It's we who struggle against nature. It flows, balances and creates. We fight, struggle and try to control.

Nature gives and loses nothing. Humans take and lose everything.

Possession exists in the mind. It is only within your mind that you believe you are entitled to an object just because you traded it for parts of a tree that we chopped down and colored.

When you free your mind of possession, anxiety over losing things disappears. You cannot lose anything if you never owned anything.

The Myth of Freedom:

What is freedom? Is it the physical act of not being in prison? Is it being free to do whatever you please regardless of the consequences?

Nelson Mandela, the former president of South Africa, spent 18 years in prison as a political prisoner before he became president.

He never felt like a prisoner. Even after he was released, he never acted out of hate, anger or revenge. He left his prison days in prison and never allowed it to eat at him. He was always free, even in prison.

He did not allow his imprisonment to destroy his character, soul or being. In fact, he rose above all obstacles and even became president.

The Queen of England, however, must always be careful of what she says, what she does, how she acts and who she becomes. She is not free to be herself. She can only be what is expected of her. Is she free?

You may not be in a physical prison; but the question is, are you in a mental one? Do you worry about losing your things or money? Do you worry about the people in your life? Worry comes from fear and fear imprisons the mind.

Fear is fueled by ignorance and it sparks discrimination. People fear what they don't know. We fear our neighbors, we fear strangers, and we fear foreigners. It seems like there is always something to fear. How can we ever be free?

True freedom exists from within. If we are free from fear, we are free regardless of our circumstances.

Freedom from fear doesn't mean being careless and aggressive. It doesn't mean, "I'm not afraid of anything so I'm going to be as careless and stupid as possible."

Freedom allows the mind to be at peace. Freedom is not physical. You are not free of this world or of this life. You are not free from the needs of your body. You will still need to find food, water and relieve yourself. True freedom is a state of mind, not a physical state.

You can break up with someone and be physically free from them, but spend hours a day thinking about them. You are not free of them even though you are physically separated.

When people experience a trauma, just because the event is over and they are physically away from it doesn't mean that they are free of it.

Some people believe that they are free because they live in a free country like America. However, they are constantly worrying about losing their income. They are worrying about losing their things. They fear people on the streets or their neighbors. How can they be free?

Janis Joplin sang, "Freedom's just another word for nothing left to lose." If you want to be free, you must remember that you don't own anything. When you are free from possessions, you are free from the fear of losing them.

The only real freedom that exists is the freedom from worry, fear and belongings. You might say, "You don't know my life, I have many things to worry about." I don't believe that statement.

Your worry is for you, not for anyone else. It does not help anyone, including you. How can you worrying in your head possibly help your situation, family member or problem? All it does is cause your body to go through stress. Chronic stress can make you sick.

So even though you have many things to worry about, soon you will have an added thing to worry about when your health begins to fail. Worrying about your health will make you sicker. Therefore, worrying is never the answer to any problem.

When the mind is at peace, there is freedom. Freedom from fear and worry is the only way to create peace in the mind.

WHAT NOW?:

How many of us actually believe that we were placed on this planet to accumulate things manufactured in factories that are designed to give us a false sense of self, security, happiness and worth?

It's okay to have things you enjoy. It's okay to take pleasure in things as long as we don't link our sense of self with them.

You are not your purse, your shoes, your car, house or anything else you can purchase.

If you lost all of those things, you would still be you. In fact, even if you lost your legs in a car accident, you would not stop being you.

You are not defined by what you have. When you lose your sense of self in things, they begin to own you.

It's just a car. It's metal, rubber, plastic and an assortment of other things that have been attached together and painted. Is it worth your life, health or happiness?

You are the one who gives it value. There are people who have purchased what you have purchased, but they don't place as much value on it. There's a saying, "one person's junk is another person's treasure." And vice versa.

The individual determines value. A ring that might be worth $500 to a thief, might feel priceless to you.

Some values are determined collectively. I call this Conditioned Collective Agreement. This is when we all decide to believe something as a group and we act as if it is truth even if we don't agree with it.

For instance, we all believe that little colorful paper holds value and we can trade it for food, clothes and other things. We all agree with it and act as if it's true even though, technically speaking, we didn't agree to it. I didn't agree that money would be valuable and yet I use it in life as if it is. I agree with my actions.

We collectively agree with our actions. We may not individually agree but we do subconsciously through conditioning. We all act as if it is true.

We all agree that these particular pieces of paper are very important. We kill for it, lie for it, steal for it, and betray each other, all for paper.

Say we acquire a large amount of these papers and we buy many things with them. Then what?

We want what we want because we don't have it. Have you ever wanted something so much that you believed you would be happy if you had it only to find yourself bored or tired of it months later?

Then your mind begins to focus on the next thing that will make you happy, and the next thing after that and so on.

It is a never-ending game of having the next thing you don't have. However, it seems like regardless of how much we accumulate, we still feel empty.

Happy people do not need many things. People who accumulate things to be happy will never be happy.

Do you really believe that metal, plastic, rubber and glue will make you happy? It may give you temporary pleasure, but will it truly make you happy?

They are meaningless gadgets marketed to make you believe that you will find happiness if you purchased them.

I took a marketing class in college and learned some interesting tools for selling products.

I learned that there are special techniques marketing companies use to convince people that they NEED a product. There are emotions to play on, weaknesses to press and lies to verbalize repeatedly to make them feel as facts.

We learned how to tap into people's fears and create a sense of urgent need for a product. We learned the different range of emotions to aim for and the appropriate words that trigger those fears and emotions in people.

I learned that companies use psychology to make people feel as though they are unhappy, unsecure, boring or unintelligent unless they buy their product.

These tactics create Fear-Based Wants. There is a fear of being poor or looking poor, a fear of being unhappy, a fear of losing someone or something, a fear of instability or a fear of not being safe.

Companies tap into our general fears and then offer their products as the "solution". We rarely want something that's not a Fear-Based Want.

The you that knows it is complete doesn't need a ninth pair of shoes or a thousand-dollar handbag. That's a Fear-Based Want. It's a fear of feeling poor, feeling less than others or a fear of unhappiness. Perhaps it's another fear; either way, you know deep down inside that you don't need any of those things.

Our culture has been conditioned to believe that owning things is crucial to our happiness. The so-called "American Dream" that has been grinded into people's sub-consciousness is all about owning a home. It is this myth that has contributed to the current economic collapse of the United States.

People ran out and bought homes they could not afford. The banks were careless and lent people money who could not afford their homes. Then the banks turned around and sold those bad investments to Wall Street. So, when everyone who couldn't afford their homes suddenly couldn't pay the banks anymore, the domino effect crashed banks, Wall Street, the United States and all the other countries who had invested in the United States.

There are many factors responsible in this current crisis; however, it all begins with the people who took out loans to purchase homes they could not afford.

We all want the good things in life. But have you ever asked yourself why you want the things you want? Are you giving into a myth? Do you just want it because you believe that everyone else wants it? Do you want it because you believe it will make you happy?

Most of the time, we don't want the thing itself, we want the emotion we believe we will have when we purchase it.

What is it that you truly want? That specific house and that specific car or the happiness and safety you believe you will feel when you have it?

When you strip all of those physical things away, you will find that what you really want is a myth.

There is no security, independence, stability, ownership or a magical product that will make you happy forever. The only thing that is real is happiness.

We all appear to want different things, when really we all have different Fear-Based Wants because we have different fears.

Our main want, happiness, is universal. We all want to be happy but we have been confused about how to attain happiness.

We chase after myths, filling our lives with metals, plastic, rubber and other elements when what we truly seek is the happiness we believe we will experience once we have them.

QUOTE:
"Let us not look back in anger or forward in fear, but around in awareness." -James Thurber, *Lanterns & Lances*

"Consciousness"

"What you do speaks so loudly that I cannot hear what you say." -Ralph Waldo Emerson

We walk a subconsciously chosen path: one of reaction, blame, reasons, cycles, miscommunication, misunderstandings and limiting beliefs.

It is a path doomed to go on forever because of our unawareness of it or resistance to acknowledge it. When we finally become aware, we can then begin to alter our lives in miraculous ways.

The path is what we call life, the events that take place between birth and death.

Countless studies have found that a very large percentage of all human behavior is habitual. From the moment you wake up to the moment you go to sleep at night, up to 90 percent of how you behave is based on how you usually behave.

When we typically think of habits, we think of smoking, drinking or biting nails. Those are obvious habits, and we know about them. There are habits, however, that we don't even realize we have.

We use habit to create order in our lives. It gives us a false sense of stability. Sometimes, those habits can be negative, depressing, unhealthy or unwise. Nevertheless, we have them because we subconsciously created them.

Awareness goes against habit. It is what is required to see habits, break old habits and form new, positive ones.

When we consciously make a decision or perform an act, we are aware that we are doing it. We hold the ability to adjust our actions at any point in time. We can choose to stop what we are doing and do something else.

Habits are the programs in our Autopilot lives.

There are two mental modes in Life: Conscious and Autopilot. These modes have two types of actions: Action and Reaction.

We must be fully conscious that we are fully conscious in our waking life. To be unaware of this is to be on Autopilot. Our lives on Autopilot are full of bad habits, cycles and suffering.

Most of us live our lives on Autopilot. All actions on Autopilot are reactive. We say or do things as a reaction to other people or other things.

This is very common. Someone or something makes us upset and we react without a second thought. We feel as though our power or control were threatened so we react immediately to regain it.

We do it because it gives us a false sense of power, when in reality we have surrendered our power.

When our actions are reactions to others, we lose our control over the situation and ourselves.

Many times people do the opposite of what is asked of them in defiance of the other person. They feel as though the other person is trying to control them so they act out. What they don't realize is that the acting out is also a form of control. The other person is still controlling us, just not directly.

We are no longer doing something we choose to do. Either the act or the motive behind the act has changed. The act is no longer authentic with who we are. It's reactive.

It's not a conscious action but a reaction with the specific purpose of defiance or revenge. The action is no longer our own but a result of someone else. Most importantly, the action is no longer coming from us and yet it directly affects our life.

If I go home from work angry with my boss and rage against my family, drink alcohol to numb my feelings or stay in an angry mood all day, I have voluntarily given my power over to my boss. In this situation, the power my boss holds over me is immense. He or she has the power to make me rage, drink and destroy my relationships. That is far too much power to grant to anyone.

On Autopilot, you are controlled by a part of yourself that does things without conscious thought. Unfortunately, the things that it does are never to your benefit. Sometimes it may seem like it is filling a need you have, but ultimately it destroys things in your life. It destroys relationships, opportunities and possibilities of happiness.

Some people call it ego, others call it pride, but it doesn't matter what name you give to it - the important thing to understand is that it's not conscious and therefore you are not in control.

Anytime your actions are a subconscious result of someone else's actions, you are on Autopilot. Many times, it is pain, anger and feelings of betrayal that cause people to go into Autopilot.

One day on Autopilot, with reactive responses, can cause a chain reaction of reactive responses from others, which will then cause additional reactive responses in you. Without knowing, you have set into motion a long list of chain reactions that control and change your life and relationships.

A Drop of Honey

The great Armenian writer Hovhannes Tumanyan, wrote a poem called, A Drop of Honey, that illustrates this point exactly.

In the poem, a shepherd walks into the nearby village market with his dog to buy a jar of honey. The peasant shopkeeper pours the honey into the jar, and a drop of honey falls to the ground.

A fly sits on the honey and the shopkeeper's cat instinctively jumps up and smacks the fly. The shepherd's dog reactively jumps on the cat and grabs it by the neck, killing it.

The shopkeeper, upset at his poor cat's demise, picks up a bat, hits the dog over the head and kills the dog. The shepherd becomes outraged that the shopkeeper killed his faithful friend and hits the shopkeeper over the head with his cane, killing him.

The villagers begin screaming, people pour out of their houses to see what had happened. They find out about the shopkeeper's death and attack the shepherd, killing him.

The shepherd's village finds out about his death and they come over for justice and vengeance. They pour onto the streets, looting, beating and killing the villagers.

When the king hears about the attack on his village, he sends soldiers into the neighboring land. However, when the neighboring land's king discovers that they are being invaded, he wages war against them, sending his army into their land.

Villages were burned, people were beaten and killed. Seasons passed and eventually years passed. Famine broke out across both lands and everyone suffered. Here is the ending to the poem:

"Famine came and brought pain to this land
A blossoming country turned into wasteland
And the people who did survive-
Kept wondering in vain
Where this enormous tragedy began."

This may sound like an outlandish story that would never actually happen but it is the perfect example of reactive response after reactive response leading to an end that no one asked for or directly chose.

How you treat others is your responsibility. No one can make you lose your integrity, act out of character or rage or become violent without your permission.

We can justify the hate, war and violence we cause on others by pointing to their behavior. But if we hate, war and react in violence, isn't our behavior justification for others to hate, war and use violence on us? When would it stop?

If we pointed the finger to those we used violence against and claimed it was their fault that we reacted as we did, then they can do the same and claim that their behavior was someone else's fault. Moreover, those people can blame others and so on. All we are left with is a series of behaviors and reactions that no one chose or wanted.

Looking at the Israeli - Palestinian conflict, each side has a reason to blame the other for their violent behavior. One can say, I'm attacking you because you attacked me, and the other can say, I attacked you because you attacked me. And so on.

Siblings often use these excuses when they are caught fighting each other. "He hit me first!" "That's because he said I was stupid." "I said you're stupid because you broke my toy." "I broke your toy because you wouldn't let me play with it." "I wouldn't let you play with it because you wouldn't let me play with your toy yesterday." Etc.

The reasons can flow back to years or even lifetimes before the actual incident. And if we go even further than that, all excuses can lead to the very beginning of time. You can blame everything on The Big Bang or God creating the universe (whichever one you believe). After all, if none of those things had happened then you would not have been born and that chain of reactions would not have occurred.

We all have a tendency to react without thinking in times of stress, tragedy, sadness or loss. If only we knew that if we just took one moment to think, we might not create an undesirable end.

If we fail to realize that our actions cause reactions in others, we will continue to create situations we don't like or want.

If only one person in that chain reaction of tragedy had just stopped and decided not to react with hate, vengeance or negativity then that unwanted end would have been avoided completely.

People find themselves in unnecessary situations frequently and wonder how they got there.

It seems as if people are not just acting without thinking, but existing without thinking, without considering and without choosing.

Why live a life you did not choose? Why live a life on Autopilot?

We have instances in our lives that require us to choose what we want to do next and how we want to react. You may not be able to choose the thing that happens to you, but you can choose how you react to it.

When an event happens that you didn't choose, you can still choose the outcome.

I had an old friend who had lost her boyfriend to another girl. She stated that she did not care for this man any longer and that she was over him. Yet most of her actions said otherwise.

She made every effort to let him know that she no longer cared for him. She worked out the things she would say to him when they accidently bumped into each other on the street. She would spend hours telling me, in full detail, about how much she no longer cared for him. Does that sound like someone who truly does not care?

She subconsciously chose to react this way because she was in pain. Did she have to react in this way? No.

In fact, her reaction caused herself far more pain than he had. She spent months of her life wasting her time trying to prove a point instead of doing something more positive and productive with her life.

Tragedies will happen. Things will always happen. It is not what happens to you that makes you who you are, but how you react to it.

We always have choices in life. If we fail to see that, we stay victims. We can choose to stay in bed and cry for days, we can choose to drown ourselves in alcohol and we can choose to stay angry all the time. However, eventually, we will get over this thing and all we will have to show for it are wasted years, bad health or a future we didn't choose.

What will happen after that? We will wake up to a future we didn't choose and continue our negative behavior because we woke up in a future we didn't choose.

My friend spent months after the break-up making sure her ex-boyfriend understood that she did not care about him any longer. When in reality, if she had not cared about him at all, she would not care if he knew that she did not care.

She felt wronged and she wanted to retaliate. It was her last effort to hurt him the way that he had hurt her. It took her a long time to realize that, but in the end, she realized it.

She was reacting to his actions and responding in Autopilot. She lost herself in the hurt and blamed him for her pain. That blame led her to cruise on Autopilot.

We should never surrender our emotions, relationships and life over to someone who has hurt us or to someone we don't like. Your life is your responsibility.

QUOTE:
"The best years of your life are the ones in which you decide your problems are your own. You do not blame them on your mother, the ecology, or the president. You realize that you control your own destiny." -Albert Ellis

---

RESPONSIBILITY:
"You will find men who want to be carried on the shoulders of others, who think that the world owes them a living. They don't seem to see that we must all lift together and pull together." -Henry Ford II

In the beginning, there was blame. The first book of the Bible, Genesis, begins with a story of blame. Adam eats the apple and blames Eve for giving it to him. Eve then blames the Serpent and they are thrown out of paradise.

Blaming is also one of the first things we learn as children. As soon as our language skills develop, we learn to blame others. Some psychologists say this is essential for human development.

Most people, however, do not stop blaming after childhood. Our society is full of groups that blame other groups for their hardships. We blame the government; we blame other races, religions and sexes.

Why is that? The answer is simple. Blame feels good. It's guaranteed to give you a short, non-lasting sensation of pleasure. However, it takes the responsibility away from us and gives us an illusion of freedom from the situation.

For example, if I'm a poor child growing up in a poor neighborhood I can always use that as a reason for my failures or excuses as to why I don't even try.

If I go for a job interview and I don't get the job, I can blame my upbringing and not feel so bad about myself. After all, it's not my fault, that's how I was raised.

My environment was poor, I didn't have many opportunities, and so if I don't succeed it's not my fault.

Blame may make you feel good for a short time, but it won't fix your problems. Regardless of how much I blame my poor neighborhood, it does not change my environment or my failures.

Blame can sometimes make your problems appear worse. When you blame, you become a victim. Your problem becomes bigger than it was because it's now something or someone else's fault.

When we lose our responsibility for ourselves, we lose our internal compass and eventually ourselves.

Blame is a weakness; it's also compulsive and addictive. It may be natural for human development, but it is also a roadblock. No one has progressed or succeeded in life by using blame.

Most people feel as though they are victims of something greater. They feel helpless to change or stop it. It's in their genes, it's from their environment, their culture, their religion, etc. It's always something else; something greater.

We live in a society of self-created victims who do not realize that they have victimized themselves. We take our own power away and blame others for it.

We reward and honor people for telling the truth and owning up to their mistakes, and yet we chronically blame any chance we get.

There are two cards in The Blame Game: Blame and Victim. Anytime we pull out the Blame card, we simultaneously pull out the Victim card.

If someone else is responsible for our misfortune, our unhappiness or our life, that means we are not. If we give away the blame, we give away the responsibility and the power to make it right. We are now victims; victims of traffic, victims of a horrible boss, mother, spouse, the weather, etc.

Since it wasn't our fault, it's not up to us to clean it up. We let ourselves off the hook. It's an easy way out. After all, we were victims of our terrible boss/mom/spouse.

We have been wronged and, on top of that, we don't have the power to clean it up. It all resides with the other person. We have just given away all our power.

We have freed ourselves of responsibility. That, however, comes with a price: stress, unhappiness and powerlessness. We have allowed ourselves to become victims. We have caused ourselves stress and unhappiness.

There is a difference between blame and responsibility: Blame is passive, responsibility is active.

When we are finished blaming, there is nothing left to do but be angry, upset, stressed or depressed. When we take responsibility, we take charge.

If we know that blame is childish, why do we still do it as adults? Why do we do negative things if we know that they are bad or immature?

Blame is a habit. It is a product of being on Autopilot. Conscious people, who make decisions not out of habit, do not blame other factors for their decisions.

Some of us, however, can get addicted to blame. This goes beyond a habit. It becomes a chronic condition. In this state, we no longer accept any form of responsibility for anything we do. Our whole life is a result of everything else; our ancestors, parents, genes, astrology sign, culture, religion, environment and the government. Everything is to be blamed for how our lives turned out, except us. This is when it has crossed over to a chronic condition.

How can a negative behavior become a chronic condition?

We emotionally gain something from all behavior. Whether it's the false sense of power we get when we rage at each other or the responsibility we give up when we blame; we receive something in return for our bad behavior or else we would stop doing it.

Evolution Theory's Natural Selection dictates that helpful traits for survival become more common in a population, and harmful traits become rarer. In other words, if a trait is not useful for survival, it eventually dies out.

Darwin, of course, was talking about physical traits but the same can be said about emotional and mental ones as well. So how can so many useless bad habits survive?

Some people blame, some love to argue all the time and others complain chronically. All these things also cause stress, which can lead to many chronic conditions within the body. Apart from being annoying and unpleasant to those around them, it is also unhealthy.

Feelings can produce a "high" that even narcotics can't recreate. People can become addicted to the feelings they receive when they blame, argue or complain. It becomes compulsive, something that cannot be managed or controlled.

The human brain is the largest pharmacy. There are more than a million chemicals in your brain. Some are over a hundred times more powerful than cocaine.

Different emotions can trigger different chemicals. These chemicals can be just as addictive as narcotics.

Emotions triggered by gambling, sex, violence, love, sports, etc, can become addictive because they activate an excitable chemical that can cause a rush or high in the individual.

Repeated behavior caused by "fun" chemicals can very easily become habits without the individual's knowledge. Because the action produces such a stimulating feeling, we may not realize how often we do it. Social scientists believe that it takes 21 days of repeated action to form a new habit.

If we fall ill for more than three weeks and become depressed because of it, it will be much harder for us to jump out of it. If we form a habit of it, we must consciously make the effort to stop the old habit or start a new one.

Unfortunately, most of the time, we don't create habits consciously. Habits are created as a reactive response to something that "happens" to us.

We fall ill so we become depressed and stay depressed. We lose our job and we take up drinking to numb the pain. We take up smoking as a reaction to stress. We create new habits as reactions to things.

Autopilot only reinforces Autopilot behavior. It creates more bad habits out of reactive responses. It feeds itself.

So what must we do first?

The first thing we must understand is that we humans create reactive habits and those habits, behaviors and actions drive our lives in a direction we didn't choose or want.

The first step is awareness. We must be aware of these things. The first step is also the awareness of responsibility.

When we are aware, we choose the event, our response and the outcome. If we cannot choose the event, like an accident or death, we can still choose our response and therefore the outcome.

Many times, we lose ourselves in an event and forget that the event is not the outcome; our response to the event is the outcome.

Whether the event is chosen or not, your response is your response-ability. No one else carries the responsibility. You can't control the traffic jam, the accidents or other things, but you can control how you react to them.

There are happy people in traffic jams, singing loudly in their cars and dancing in their seats. There are people who dance in the rain.

There is no changing a traffic jam. You can choose to be stressed, yell, scream, and honk your horn or you can relax, take the time to think, listen to the radio, call and talk to someone you haven't spoken to in a while. Whether you choose to scream, cry or sing loudly in your car, you're stuck. You can't control the event, but you can control your response.

Your response is the difference between a negative experience and a positive experience. It is not the event that makes your experience positive or negative, it is your response to it. Because of this, you always have the power to control the outcome.

When you go home that day, you will either remember the awful traffic jam from hell or the one that gave you the opportunity to catch up on your audiotapes, your phone calls or your meditation.

If you react out of habit or without thinking, the outcome will be determined for you.

The Power of Choice

Somaly Mam doesn't know how old she is. She was a Cambodian orphan who never knew her parents.

She was abused at an orphanage during her childhood and forced into marriage with an older man. She was later sold to a brothel where pimps and clients constantly beat, raped and abused her.

Following the murder of her friend, she escaped the brothel and vowed to dedicate the rest of her life to helping other sex slaves find freedom.

Since then, she has helped in the escape and healing of sex slaves in Cambodia, Vietnam and Laos through her nonprofit organizations, AFESIP (translated as "Acting for Women in Distressing Circumstances") and the Somaly Mam Foundation.

She is a speaker and activist working with government officials to lobby for the passage of anti-trafficking laws. She also solicits other former slaves and celebrity spokespeople to talk about sexual slavery.

Since her escape, Somaly has helped more than 4,000 former sex slaves find freedom and the opportunity to create a better life.

Somaly did not have the choice in becoming a sex slave; that was the event. However, she controlled her response and the outcome.

She could have chosen to escape and cry all day, wondering why this awful tragedy had to happen to her. She could have become depressed, lonely, angry and anxious and drowned her pain in alcohol or drugs.

After she escaped, she chose not to suffer any longer. Instead of choosing to stay in bed all day and curse God for her bad luck, she chose to make the most of her experience.

She could have very easily stayed angry. She could have been lost in negative thoughts and just wondered why of all people it had to happen to her.

She chose to make her experience a positive one. She chose to empower herself through her experience and she received the ultimate freedom. Many slaves escape their captures but remain emotionally and mentally enslaved.

Somaly chose not to allow her abusers to control her emotions, thoughts and life. Once she was physically free, she was free.

Instead, she uses her energies to help others find freedom and the chance to live the life they choose.

Awareness comes with responsibility. If you are aware of your actions, you are responsible for them. This is the first step. You must choose your life by choosing your outcomes.

It's important to note that we all make mistakes even when we are aware. Mistakes don't only happen on Autopilot. Even when we consciously make decisions, we can still make mistakes.

Mistakes should not be feared or avoided. They are a very important part of life. Without mistakes, human kind would not have advanced. We must know what doesn't work, in order to know what does work. This is how we grow.

Thomas Edison, when asked about inventing the light bulb, said: "I did not fail 3,000 times; I've just found 3,000 ways that won't work."

Each mistake holds a valuable lesson. That lesson is lost the moment we blame other factors. If Thomas Edison had blamed other factors for his mistakes, or chosen to give up because he made mistakes, we would not have had the light bulb.

Mistakes carry lessons. If we have missed the lesson, then we have missed an opportunity for growth.

QUOTE:

"We have not passed that subtle line between childhood and adulthood until... we have stopped saying 'It got lost,' and say, 'I lost it'." -Sidney J. Harris, *On the Contrary*

"The Human Drama"

"Don't believe everything you hear – even in your own mind." -Daniel G. Amen, M.D.

Research indicates that we have an average of 60,000 thoughts per day and about 80 percent of those thoughts are negative.

That means only 20 percent of our daily thoughts actually focus on the positive things in our lives.

Most of the time, we think about what we don't have, how much we want something or someone to be different, how much we want a different house or car or job, how much we want more money, how much we want a flatter stomach or bigger muscles. We seem to be focusing more on the lacks and the negatives in our lives.

How can we appreciate what we do have if we are constantly bombarding our brains with things we don't have or things we do have but don't want?

What effect do you think this constant negative thinking will have on our emotions, body, relationships and lives?

Is it going to help us appreciate the people in our lives that we struggle to change? Is it going to help us appreciate the job and boss we hate? Is it going to help us appreciate the life we keep wishing would be different?

How much of what we think actually affects our lives?

A classmate of mine told me about a certain type of meditation he had tried where he was locked in an empty room for a week.

The point of the exercise was to exist without any outside stimulation. He had access to a bathroom and was given three meals a day. Other than that, he was not allowed to leave the room, talk with anyone or do anything else. All he had to do was just exist.

He told me that the first few hours were very joyful. His mind was calm and he felt happy about trying the new method of meditation.

After a few hours, he began thinking to himself. He wondered why no one had come to check up on him. Then he started to think that they were all cons and they were just taking his money and offering nothing in return. He felt like an idiot. He had been deceived.

He began to rage. He started screaming and banging against the walls for someone to let him out. After a little bit of time, when he had calmed down, one of the monks came to the door with his last meal for the night.

The monk asked him how he was doing. He began to talk about how angry and upset he was. The monk asked him if he had felt that way during the whole time.

He told him that for the first few hours he was happy. He felt good and blissful. The monk asked him what had changed. "Everything in the room is the same." Why was he happy one moment and angry the next? Nothing had changed.

He told me that he had learned a very powerful lesson about listening to the voice in his head and how we humans have a tendency to over dramatize and fuel drama when we are left alone in our own minds.

The drama that we encounter in life is created from our own minds. We burden our minds with the weight of our thoughts. Some thoughts are carefree and feel light while others drag our emotions down, make us feel terrible and affect our actions toward others.

To someone else, you are just being. They are completely unaware that there is a whole other world in your mind.

Imagine if there was another person locked in that empty room with my former classmate.

Imagine that they are sitting quietly in an empty room and one of them looks over to see the other smiling and peaceful. Moments later, he gets up and starts screaming and banging the walls.

The change happened inside. One thought led to another and another until he became so furious that he could not contain himself. Did anyone else cause this? No. He caused it.

We all have been known to do it. We get upset with someone and instead of talking with them and sorting it out, we stay in our own minds and make ourselves furious.

You start to think about it and the more you think about it, the more furious you get. The more furious you get, the more reasons you find to be furious. Suddenly you get to the point where you think, "How dare they treat me like this?"

Blame is thrown around, you become a victim and suddenly you are furious because you have been wronged.

At this point, you have been left inside your own head so long that you've reached the point of no return. Heaven help that person if they call you at that moment.

It doesn't matter what that person says or does anymore. You have decided that you are right and they are wrong.

Communication is hindered because we are too busy in our own minds to hear others. Unfortunately, many things get lost because of this and we lose potentially great relationships because we don't listen to others when they speak.

The voice inside our head is always thinking, judging and analyzing. When someone speaks, it's hard to listen.

You are having a conversation with someone and you're listening to the interpretation from the voice inside your head and not the other person.

"Is this person right or wrong? Is this person smart or crazy? Hmm, I think I like this person. What are they talking about? He has a funny nose."

Large parts of our conversations are misheard. Most of the time, people only hear half of the things you say. But they remember their interpretation of what you said, not what you actually said.

Have you ever had a fight with someone who tried to convince you that you said something you are completely positive you didn't say? Are they remembering what you said or what they think you meant?

You said something and they took their self-created meaning from what you said and stored that away.

We are running around with self-created meanings, trying to make other people understand our meanings.

The second you speak, the other person interprets and creates meaning. Meanings get stored away in our minds and attach themselves to memories.

What we choose to believe and what we choose to store in our minds can be the difference between happiness and suffering.

Try actively listening to the voice. You'll notice that instead of projecting your thoughts, it influences your thoughts. Instead of saying what you're feeling, it works to convince you of things.

We must be aware of it if we want to be able to communicate clearly with others. You don't have to believe everything it tells you, you just have to be aware.

Some people confuse it with intuition.
Intuition is a feeling. The voice inside your head is a vocalized coach. It coaches you based on your fears and anxieties. It's very much like a tape recorder that plays back your fears, negative thoughts and the criticisms you've picked up along the way.

You don't have to fight it; you just have to be aware of it. If you are aware then you don't have to believe everything it says. Moreover, if you have the freedom to refuse to believe everything it says, you are free from its hold over you.

Weight of the Mind

Two monks were traveling down a muddy road when they met a young girl who was unable to cross the muddy road. She asked for the monks' help.

The first monk shook his head and told the girl that monks aren't allowed to touch women.

"I will carry you," said the second monk. Lifting her in his arms, he carried her over the mud.

The first monk did not speak again until that night when they reached a lodging temple. Then, he no longer could restrain himself. "We monks aren't allowed to touch females," he said. "Why did you carry her?"

The second monk said, "I may have picked her up and carried her across the road, but I set her down. You are still carrying her."

What are you carrying in your mind?

QUOTE:
"Be careful of your thoughts, for your thoughts inspire your words. Be careful of your words, for your words precede your actions. Be careful of your actions, for your actions become your habits. Be careful of your habits, for your habits build your character. Be careful of your character, for your character decides your destiny." - Chinese proverb

---

SELF-TALK:
"The inner speech, your thoughts, can cause you to be rich or poor, loved or unloved, happy or unhappy, attractive or unattractive, powerful or weak." -Ralph Charell

The voice inside your head is generally very negative and mean toward both yourself and others. We already know what the negative, inaccurate inner conversations can do to our relationships with others and our lives. However, the continuous negative Self-Talk can also alter your sense of self and the world around you.

This is how it works: Self-Talk (what you tell yourself every day) affects your Self-Image (your beliefs and feelings about yourself), which in turn affects your Actions (the things you do day to day), which in turn affects your Self-Talk. This cycle must be changed in our favor.

Continuous negative Self-Talk will never make you feel good about yourself and it will affect your actions which will then reinforce your negative Self-Talk.

If we don't make a conscious decision to stop and shift, we will repeat this cycle for the rest of our lives.

So, how do we first begin to shift? Now that we know we are conscious and aware, we must be conscious and aware that we talk to ourselves every day. Once we discover what the conversation is, then we can take a step forward and begin the process of shifting.

What do you frequently tell yourself? In moments of stress, in moments of pain or failure, what is the conversation in your mind?

Autosuggestion is the process used for positive or negative change within the mind and/or body. The French psychologist Émile Coué wrote about the theory and practice of autosuggestion.

He used autosuggestion to explain the power of suggestion and the effects it caused on the physical symptoms of his patients. He believed that the thoughts and beliefs of a person affected the body.

Coué noticed that when he spoke positively about a specific medication before giving it to the patient, the medicine was more effective.

His patients experienced more pain when they were told a procedure would hurt. He noticed that the power of suggestion had a powerful affect on the body. Headaches would sometimes go away after taking a painkiller, but before the painkiller could actually start acting on its own.

Therefore, when the brain expects a certain reaction in the body, it usually creates it. If the brain expects the body to feel pain, the body feels pain.

We all know this to be true because of our dreams. We have all had dreams where we felt physical pain because we were hurt in our dreams but in reality, we were safely lying in our beds.

I once dreamt that I was burned by fire and I could feel the pain of the burn on my skin. When I woke up, there was no fire. So how did I feel the pain?

When your brain expects something, it reacts accordingly.

This influence of the mind on the body can be used in a positive way to improve the way a person feels (mentally or physically).

Autosuggestion is a process we use to train our subconscious mind to believe something. If we continually tell someone that they are sick and that they look sick, the person will subconsciously use autosuggestion to make the self believe that he is sick.

If you walked up to someone who was healthy and said, "Are you feeling okay? You don't look so well." You will psychologically alter their thinking. They will now wonder if they are okay. They will scan their body for aches or pains and even manifest them.

We can use autosuggestion consciously in our favor. We usually have a habit of telling ourselves negative information, bombarding our subconscious mind with negativity we eventually end up believing.

You can use autosuggestion by presenting your mind with repetitive thoughts (negative or positive), until those thoughts become internalized.

Autosuggestion can be used deliberately to help you shift your thoughts and beliefs. However, it is also an unintentional process. Whether you realize it or not, you are using autosuggestion to make yourself believe things.

The main thoughts in a person's conscious mind, if repeated over a long period, can train the person's subconscious mind to arrange their beliefs according to those thoughts.

For instance, if a child is continually told that he is stupid, when he becomes an adult, the voice inside his head will continue the abuse even if the people have been removed from his life.

The constant repetition of the abuse will influence the actions of the individual, which will then affect the Self-Talk.

All these factors make relationships very difficult since the basis of any relationship is communication. It makes it very difficult to listen to each other when the voice inside our heads is talking at the same time.

Instead of acting as a loud speaker to your thoughts, it acts as a separate entity that influences your thoughts and emotions.

With all the miscommunication, inaccurate judging and misunderstanding, it takes far more effort and energy to get along with each other.

You choose what you tell yourself. Why choose the negative?

QUOTE:

"Doing more of what doesn't work won't make it work any better." - Charles J. Givens

---

WHERE ARE YOU COMING FROM?

"To see what is in front of one's nose needs a constant struggle." -George Orwell

We already know that we can consciously choose the decisions we make and we must take responsibility for those decisions. We also understand how our internal Self-Talk can influence and alter our actions.

The next step is to go deep into where we are coming from when we perform those actions.

Sometimes we can wake up from Autopilot and make a fully conscious decision, but still find ourselves unhappy and stressed.

We must understand where our actions are stemming from if we want to make conscious decisions. Is it from a peaceful and happy place or a place of spite, vengeance, anger, frustration and stress?

Humans have an unconscious ability to spread happiness when they experience it themselves. Happiness has a habit of expanding, both within the person and to those around the person.

Those of us who are angry, mean, manipulative or hostile are not happy. Happy people don't feel compelled to ridicule, criticize or make fun of others; those are characteristics of someone who is unhappy.

Unhappiness can stem from suffering, stress, frustration, etc.

I knew a group of girls in high school who had a tendency of being mean toward other girls. They constantly made rude remarks and laughed at other people.

A few years after high school, I ran into an old friend of mine who told me that one of those girls used to live in an abusive home and another had lost her mother at a very young age.

I learned that they were hurting inside when they were causing pain in others. It was hurt and suffering they were spreading. If I were wiser then, I would have felt compassion toward them in high school, instead of feeling anger.

It is now I understand that people are suffering inside. Suffering is what manifests when we don't know how to properly release our pain. We all have different ways of releasing pain, and sometimes we release it through negativity toward others or ourselves.

Those girls who released their pain negatively sparked a negative reaction in other people. That, unfortunately, added more fuel to the fire and kept the vicious cycle spinning.

If someone is hurting inside and we react negatively to their negativity, it only strengthens their continued negativity.

When groups of people are discriminated against and they take out their frustrations violently, it only reinforces the discrimination.

Let us pretend for a moment that you believe all women are angry and violent so you discriminate against them. I, as a woman, become frustrated with your hate and discrimination and I become verbally abusive and violent toward you.

My reactions reinforce the hate you have for me, which in turn, reinforces the anger I feel toward you.

This vicious cycle must be broken through compassion. Dr. Martin Luther King Jr., leader of the civil rights movement in America, said:

"Through violence you may murder the liar, but you cannot murder the lie, nor establish the truth. Through violence, you may murder the hater, but you do not murder hate. In fact, violence merely increases hate.

Returning violence for violence multiplies violence, adding deeper darkness to a night already devoid of stars. Darkness cannot drive out darkness: only light can do that. Hate cannot drive out hate: only love can do that."

When people are angry, mean, aggressive, pretentious or cruel, it means they are in pain.

Those of us who are the hardest to love, are the ones who need it the most.

Reacting with negativity, anger or violence to negativity, anger and violence will never stop negativity, anger and violence.

This may sound very simple but how many times have we shouted at a shouting man or used violence as an answer to violence?

If we all understand that we all share the same pain but for different reasons, perhaps we can begin to heal by exercising compassion.

We must look at how we function as human beings and why we do what we do. Perhaps if we understand each other better, we may decrease discrimination, anger and violence and increase compassion.

There are people in the world you can justify hating. Our minds divide, separate and label. We put people in groups and then label those groups. It becomes much easier for us to judge others when we do that.

When we meet someone on the street, we immediately place them in one of our categories and act accordingly.

There is no opportunity to know the individual. The individual does not exist any longer, but are now a part of a larger group you either like or dislike. There is no room for understanding or acceptance.

What can we do now? How do we begin to shift? We must look within ourselves first to answer the question: where are we coming from?

There is a human tendency to hide something about ourselves we don't want others to know. Unfortunately, these things can be obvious to others because it is the exact opposite emotion of what we are trying to express.

Psychology teaches us that people who routinely act superior and have a superiority complex, generally feel very low about themselves. They usually project their feelings of inferiority onto people they see as beneath them, possibly for the same reasons they themselves may have been ostracized. For example, they may view most, possibly all, others as "ugly" or "stupid" and beneath themselves.

People, who display themselves as "above" others actually believe that they are in fact lower than others. This is why they feel the need to act as the opposite, so that others will not know their "secret."

Happy people do not feel the need to "lower" others. In fact, happy people feel compelled to make others happy as well.

People who normally show one thing generally feel the opposite about themselves. Those reactions are coming from a lack: a lack of love, security, intelligence, happiness. There is something that you feel you need to compensate for.

The more you overdo something, the less you believe you have of it.

A person who believes that they are intelligent does not need to put their intelligence on display. By convincing others that you are intelligent, you in turn convince yourself. It's almost as though we think that if we can convince enough people, then we can convince ourselves as well. After all, those people can't all be wrong.

A man who overly displays his masculinity does not feel like a man internally. In fact, most things in life only remind him that he needs to be a stronger man. He acts even more brutish because, in his mind, they are "attacks" to his manhood.

I knew a boy in high school who was very athletic. He was strong and very masculine. He had a mean sense of humor and sometimes I overheard him say negative things about other people.

I found out from a mutual friend of ours that he had a very dominating father who called him "weak" and a "girl" when he cried as a child. He was raised in a house where he wasn't allowed to show emotion because it meant that he was a girl.

This had an enormous effect on the psyche of this boy. He was seventeen years old, walking around with his father's voice in his head constantly telling him he was weak. He judged situations and things based on whether it made him look weak or strong. It controlled his entire life.

He became an athlete to "look" like a man. He lifted weights and spent hours in the gym to look like a "real" man. He even verbally abused other boys who appeared to be weak so that he appeared bigger and stronger.

He spent most of his days reacting to his father's voice in his head. When he believed that he appeared "weak," he became crueler or worked-out harder.

His actions were a direct reaction to the statement, "I am weak."

We walk around with inferiority statements we are trying to hide or eliminate. These statements are not facts, but we believe them as if they are facts.

We overcompensate for whatever it is we feel we lack. Those of us who overly display our intellect live with the statement, "I am stupid." We feel the constant need to display our intelligence; otherwise, people will know that we are stupid.

If you and I received a "B" on our test, we would be content. However, if they received a "B," it would mean so many negative things about them. It would mean for them that they are "stupid," that so-and-so was right about them, that they're a "loser," etc. It shatters the image they have worked so hard to create and that can be devastating.

My overly athletic friend was not weak. People who excessively display their intellect are not stupid. They usually believe that they are.

It is okay to be athletic and smart, but when we do it to reinforce an image of ourselves, it becomes a problem. Then you are living your life to compensate for something and not because it makes you happy.

Thoughts, feelings, behaviors and habits can be changed to our liking at any time we choose. Most of the time, we don't choose them to our benefit.

The question is: where are you coming from? When you communicate with others, are you coming from a place of love and compassion or are you coming from a place of hurt and anger?

When you do what you do, are you coming from a place of happiness or overcompensation?

Most actions come from a place of fear. A fear of being discovered, a fear of appearing weak, a fear of looking bad.

When you are buying a car, are you buying it from a place of fear? Maybe you want to show the world that you are rich in fear of others thinking that you are poor. Maybe you want to show others that you are secure, fun or happy.

We all want to be happy. That is a universal human desire. Just like suffering is a universal human emotion shared by all. Unfortunately, we sometimes spend more energy trying to "look" happy to others rather than actually being happy.

You are a three-dimensional person. Most importantly, you see yourself as a three-dimensional person. You feel happy, sad and angry, you are loving, mean, kind, careless, etc.

What if I met you when you were angry; would I be accurate to conclude that you are a mean person?

We only see snapshots of people. Even the people we see every day are only snapshots.

We each contain worlds within ourselves. Worlds full of dreams, hopes, aspirations and a desire to be happy.

People we yell at, rage against, hurt or even kill, share two things with ourselves: They are suffering and they want to be happy.

People who aren't suffering don't yell, rage, hurt or kill others.

No happiness can ever be achieved by doing any of those things. So if you are not happy, then you are working on your suffering. You are feeding your suffering. Unfortunately, it also adds on top of others' suffering as well.

We don't have access to other people's worlds and so we can never truly know them. Even if we did have access, we can only enter and see their world through our eyes, which are tainted with our experiences, beliefs and thoughts.

You can say, "I know them." But how can you really know someone? There are so many things about yourself you don't know, how much can you know about others?

The only thing we can accurately conclude is that human beings contain multitudes we can't access in one lifetime. We're usually too busy in our own heads to even want to access them.

QUOTE:
" All violence is the result of people tricking themselves into believing that their pain derives from other people and that consequently those people deserve to be punished." -Marshall Rosenberg

---

NARCISSISM:
"Someone said of a very great egotist: `He would burn your house down to cook himself a couple of eggs.'"
-Nicolas de Chamfort

Narcissism is a form of self-obsession. Narcissists are concerned with their image rather than their selves.

It seems to be a growing epidemic in our current culture, especially with celebrities and people who idolize those celebrities.

Working for the Juvenile Probation Department for a few years, I have noticed it more and more in the youth. However, it is also very evident in adults as well.

It seems that in our culture, we are very concerned with how we appear to others. How did this make me look? Do I look caring, giving or loving? Caring, giving and loving people don't have to think about being those things, they just are. Therefore, we have lost the line between being and looking like we're being.

Narcissists are only concerned with their own goals and feelings. They usually overreact to criticism and become angry or humiliated. They can fall into narcissistic rage when another person is attacking their grandiose sense of self-worth. Their natural reaction is to rage and pull down the self-worth of others to make themselves feel superior to others.

They are easily jealous and lack empathy toward others' feelings and pain. In fact, they enjoy putting others down or watching others fail because it makes them feel better.

Narcissists can always rationalize and justify their self-centered behavior and possess very strong feelings of entitlement; in other words, they believe that they deserve great things and therefore don't care who they hurt in the process of getting those things.

Narcissists are generally in denial because they cannot allow themselves to believe anything negative about themselves. Therefore, it is very difficult for one to admit such behavior.

They have unrealistic fantasies of importance, power, beauty and achievements. In addition, when they do fail, they often have an automatic denial mechanism to downplay their inadequacies. They are generally arrogant and exaggerate their own importance. They are proud and need constant attention from others.

Narcissists feel entitled to everything and don't care to work for the things they want. They are used to instant gratification and expect immediate results or rewards to anything they do.

We are raising a generation of narcissistic children because we don't allow them to feel pain, make mistakes or earn anything they receive.

When a child feels pain, we rush to stop it. We shower them with gifts to ease the pain and make ourselves feel better. We want our children to have the best and so we give them the best to feed our own egos. We also correct their mistakes and don't allow them to fail because it makes us look bad as parents.

We do all of these things to protect our children and all we end up doing is stunting their growth as people. By making ourselves feel better and feeding our own egos, we have created a generation of children too emotionally and mentally involved in themselves to communicate or survive in our social world.

Our own narcissism is passed down to our children unbeknownst to us. The opposite behavior can also create a narcissistic child as well. Too much criticism, judgment and abuse (mental, emotion or physical) can cause a child to develop a superiority complex (arrogance, feelings of being better than others) due to their feelings of inferiority (low self-esteem, shame, feeling lower than others). The mind tries to defend the self and so it creates a false superior image to cling onto. It's an internal fight between the real self and the image of the self.

Narcissists can't be happy. It goes against their disorder. This continuous cycle of judgment, jealousy, resentment and arrogance stands in the way of happiness. They experience pleasure when they receive attention but it's only short-lived. This is why they constantly need to create drama to stay in the spotlight.

We can see this type of behavior in actors, singers, rappers, musicians, writers, producers and many other people in the entertainment industry.

Children born into fame, money or power can develop Acquired Situational Narcissism fueled by our celebrity-obsessed society. Their fans, assistants and media all play into the idea that the person is far more important than other people. This triggers an internal narcissistic crisis that might have been only a tendency, or might have been completely dormant, and helps it to become a full-blown personality disorder.

However, it is also very visible in our own lives. With many Internet social networking Websites popping up by the hundreds, we too clearly feel the need to place ourselves on display, worrying more about our image than our selves. Our current culture feeds narcissism at every turn. Reality TV, movies, the Internet, newspapers and magazines - they all act as ego-boosters.

We all have a little bit of narcissism within us. However, when it is at a point of pathology, it can greatly hinder a person's ability to relate or feel empathy toward others. Other people are only seen as audience members to their drama, tools to reach a goal or means of positive reinforcement that feed their egos.

Don't be concerned with finding the narcissist in your environment. I imagine that you are probably scanning your mind right now finding the narcissists you know.

Nevertheless, this book is not about everyone else and it is not a tool to use to judge others or make you feel better by putting others down. This book is about you.

Look within to your own behavior, thoughts and feelings. After all, even the narcissist will look at others, judge and point fingers but would never think to look within. It's far too painful and real because narcissists aren't interested in what is real, only their own image and what they want to be real.

QUOTE:
"I sit on a man's back; choking him and making him carry me, and yet assure myself and others that I am very sorry for him and wish to ease his lot by all possible means except by getting off his back." -Leo Tolstoy, *Writings on Civil Disobedience and Nonviolence*

"The Body"

"Emotion always has its roots in the unconscious and manifests itself in the body." -Irene Claremont de Castillejo

When I was twenty-one, I had a car accident that, I can now say, forever changed my life. The funny thing is that it didn't even dent my front bumper.

The incident triggered a series of events that lead to three years of suffering, sickness, revelations, epiphanies and, ultimately, enlightenment.

I suffered from dizzy spells, anxiety attacks, depression, high and low blood pressure, nausea, vertigo, large ovarian cysts. I was hospitalized, had surgery, placed on hormones and, at one point, the doctor told me that I might possibly have cancer. One after another, packed in a three-year period, illness fell upon illness.

Every health crisis I experienced caused more anxiety, panic attacks and paranoia. Every day I was afraid that something much more terrible was going to happen to me.

I spent two-and-a-half-years of my life in my house. I did not go outside and I did not drive. I spent most of that time reading, writing and pondering.

I lost my old friends, my band, my job and I lost all the things that I identified as my life. However, it was in retrospect that I realized that losing every single of those things was a blessing in disguise.

I suffered emotionally, physically and psychologically; most of which I did to myself.

When I say that I did it to myself, I mean that the majority of my illness was a result of my thoughts, feelings and actions.

Thoughts and feelings have more affect over the body than we had initially believed.

Every day, scientists are further uncovering the links between our thoughts and our health.

We know that our thoughts, feelings and beliefs affect our body to a certain extent. After all, that is how a lie detector operates.

When you lie, your pulse increases, your blood pressure changes, your sweat glands produce sweat, your breathing changes, etc.

Your body physically reacts to lying whether you realize it or not. Your body also reacts to negative thoughts.

Continuous negative thoughts can cause depression, anxiety, panic attacks and stress.

Stress does not exist out in the world; it exists internally. You cannot stumble onto stress. It does not exist in a store where you can go buy it. It exists in our internal conversation.

We cause stress for ourselves. Some things, out in the world, may be interpreted as stressful, but those things aren't stressful in themselves. We see them as stressful, we believe them to be stressful and our bodies react to them accordingly.

When you become stressed, your body releases the stress hormone Cortisol. It increases blood pressure, blood sugar and suppresses the immune system.

Chronic stress can cause serious problems to the body. High blood pressure, backaches, digestive problems, heart disease, diabetes, immune deficiencies, memory and concentration problems and it can lead to depression and anxiety disorders.

Chronic stress in children can impair developmental growth by lowering the pituitary glands that produce growth hormones.

Stress and adrenaline helped our ancestors survive terrible environments thousands of years ago. It helped us stay alive. Unfortunately, now we are killing ourselves with a tool for survival.

We become stressed in doing everyday activities from driving to shopping to working. However, those things don't cause us stress. It is rooted in our thinking.

For some people, shopping, driving and working are pleasurable experiences. Anything that causes you to feel stress can be a pleasurable experience for someone else.

Therefore, it can't be the thing, itself. It must come from our internal makeup and not from some genetic disposition that we can't control or do anything about. It is from our everyday practices.

I have dealt with anxiety and depression for years. I dealt with it in my teen years and shortly after I became ill in my twenties. Both times, I chose not to take medication for them.

I didn't think that taking a pill to stop the physiological process of anxiety would help cure the problem. It only took care of the symptoms or after effects. It didn't deal with the underlining issues that triggered the anxiety.

Instead, I chose to take the time and deal with the issues. I wasn't aware of what the issues were initially and that is why time was required to deal with them appropriately.

So many people choose to pump themselves full of drugs because it is the short and easy way. Even then, people still claim that depression symptoms don't go away when they are using anti-depressant drugs to cure them.

Are we treating the problem or just the symptoms? Instead of dealing with what is causing the anxiety and the depression, we pump ourselves full of pills to stop the physical reactions because they are convenient and easy.

I didn't take the easy road. Both times, I spent two years at home and rarely left my house because every time I stepped outside I had an anxiety attack.

Day by day, I took small steps to ease myself back into the outside world. I would take a short ten-minute trip to get coffee or run an errand. Each time I went outside and didn't have an anxiety attack, I rewarded myself internally and made myself feel good for the progress I was making. Instead of being mad at myself for not staying out longer, I rewarded myself for the time I did spend out.

I didn't allow myself to say negative things about my progress. I shifted my Self-Talk and made myself feel good and at ease. Eventually, over time, my mind calmed down and my anxiety became less and less frequent.

Emotionally speaking, the brain can't tell the difference between an experience and the memory of an experience.

The same chemical reaction happens within the brain and body when the experience is remembered.

Looking at your pet then closing your eyes and remembering your pet gives you the same loving effect in your brain. Just like thinking of an attack and experiencing an attack causes the same physiological reaction within your body. Your heart rate increases, you start sweating, you breathe faster and panic starts to set in, even if it's just a memory.

This is why a sexual fantasy can cause the body to react as if it is happening. A traumatic experience can cause the body to react with stress and anxiety as if it is actually happening as well.

Therefore, if you continuously think stressful thoughts and relive unhappy memories, your brain will react as if it is really occurring and pump more stress into your body. You can wear yourself out and cause sickness by bombarding your brain with stressful memories and thoughts.

This will also train the brain to react with stress and anxiety even when it does not call for it.

To look at this from a biological point of view, we must understand two important aspects of the brain.

The hippocampus registers the situation of experiences. It plays an important role in the formation of new memories about experienced events. For example, tiger approaching = possible death because we remember that tigers eat people.

The amygdala sends signals to other parts of the brain on whether the experience is threatening; it is the alarm bell. It plays a primary role in the processing and memory of emotional reactions. It will take in the information of the experience and ring the alarm bell if it is threatening. In the tiger situation, it will be ringing a very large alarm bell to cause panic and stress within the body so that the body can prepare to run or fight.

They work together to keep you safe and alive. The hippocampus keeps the amygdala quiet and calm so that it does not ring the alarm bell for just any situation and send a flurry of anxiety and adrenaline running through your body for no reason.

However, chronic stress causes our amygdala to become sensitive and heightened, ringing the alarm bell even when there is no threat to our lives. In addition, Cortisol, the stress hormone, eats away at the hippocampus causing it to deteriorate and become less effective in causing the amygdala to keep quiet.

So a chronically stressed person may find themselves feeling stress or anxiety for unthreatening reasons. It rewires the brain to be highly anxious for everything.

We so often forget that thoughts and feelings are not facts. Your everyday thoughts are important to the health of your overall being.

Repeated exposure to stress can build up in the brain, which then causes a negative impact on the body.

Stress and anxiety can also cause feelings of anger and frustration. New studies have shown that chronic anger leads to heart disease.

The study showed that people suffering with chronic anger have a tendency to smoke, drink and eat unhealthy which can lead to heart disease. Chronically angry people also have more adrenalin in their body and that can speed up the process of heart disease as well.

If someone is angry all the time, they are only

going to find more things to be angry about. They can blame the people around them, their job, situation or life, but that's not going to solve the problem. Since when has blame ever solved anything?

Unless they consciously shift, people who are angry all the time will continue to be angry because they have wired their brains to do so. If they change the situation, they will find something else to be angry about. If they change their spouse, they will find something with the new spouse that makes them angry.

Their anger is not a reaction to anything anyone is actually doing. Their anger is internal, personal and it creates more anger. The cycle continues and they become trapped.

This also applies to chronic complainers. Complainers will always find something to complain about. They have wired themselves to find things they are unhappy about.

If they were offered a free trip to Las Vegas, they would complain about the size of the room. In their eyes, nothing is ever as it should be, so they complain. They don't allow themselves or those around them to enjoy life or to accept things as they are. Unfortunately, that acceptance is what leads to happiness.

The good news is that it can be changed and reversed regardless of how old you are. Scientists used to believe that when the brain reached adulthood, the brain was wired and could not be changed. Scientists now believe that regardless of age, the brain can be rewired.

Neuroscientist and professor of psychology and psychiatry, Richard J. Davidson, PhD, runs the Laboratory for Affective Neuroscience in the University of Wisconsin–

Madison. For years now, he has been scientifically uncovering the architecture of emotions.

Using brain-imaging technologies, he and his team of researchers have been studying the brain structures behind anxiety, depression, addiction, happiness, resilience and, most recently, compassion.

He used "brain-mapping" in one of his studies involving employees at a biotech company. Half of the employees completed about three hours of meditation once a week. After four months, the meditating employees noticed an improvement in mood and decrease in anxiety, while their immune systems became noticeably stronger.

Davidson found that meditation produced a significant increase in activity in the part of the brain responsible for positive emotions and traits like optimism and resilience—the left prefrontal cortex. In Buddhist monks, this area lit up brightly showing activity beyond anything he and his team had ever seen.

It appears that practicing meditation regularly can wire the brain toward happiness, optimism and peace, decreasing levels of anxiety and gloominess.

His new studies on the monks measure what happens when they engage specifically in compassion. He has found that their brains show dramatic changes in two areas: increased activity in the part of the brain that floods them with well-being and in the areas of the brain involved with motor planning. The monks are not just "feeling" good; their brains have prepared their bodies to leap up and "do" good. They are ready to jump into action and do whatever they can to help relieve suffering.

He believes that compassion is mental exercise because it trains the brain for happiness.

Most people accept the idea that regular physical exercise is something they should do for the remainder of their lives. Now we can incorporate compassion into our lives as a form of mental exercises.

There is growing research suggesting that the adult brain is changeable, as opposed to becoming fixed in adolescence. What this means is that even though one may be born with a predisposition toward sadness or anxiety, the emotional floor plan can be altered toward a happier outlook.

Much like an athlete who must practice in order to keep his muscles in shape, we must practice compassion to keep ourselves mentally healthy and happy.

The brain is reprogrammable. Whether we reprogram our brain to respond with anxiety and stress or with compassion and happiness, it can be achieved through practice.

The Two Wolves

One evening, an old Cherokee told his grandson about a battle that rages within us. He said, "My son, we all have two wolves inside us, always battling.

One is evil. It is anger, envy, jealousy, greed, arrogance, resentment, lies and pride.

The other is good. It is joy, peace, love, hope, serenity, humility, kindness, empathy, generosity, truth, compassion and faith."

The grandson asked his grandfather, "Which wolf wins?"

The old Cherokee replied, "Whichever one you feed."

QUOTE:
"Some patients I see are actually draining into their bodies the diseased thoughts of their minds." -Zachary Bercovitz

----

For more on Davidson and his research please visit: http://psyphz.psych.wisc.edu/

I BELIEVE:
"The mind can cook up very subtle syndromes to throw at our bodies. -Astrid Alauda

When I was about five years old, I ran and fell into the edge of a brick wall and cracked my head open. I still have the scar on my forehead.

I don't remember feeling any pain and I didn't cry. Even as the blood gushed down my face and covered my eyes, I don't recall feeling any pain.

I was rushed to the hospital where I received stitches and I was awake and pain-free throughout the whole procedure. I even remember the doctors sewing up my forehead and talking to me in the process.

Some martial artists train for years to wire their brains not to send pain signals to their bodies when they are hit.

Women of tribal societies squat and give birth in the fields, bite off the umbilical cord and go back to work without feeling any pain.

In our western societies, we have been taught that a woman must suffer at birth. This is passed down generation to generation and because it is believed, it happens.

When we expect pain, we receive pain. However, we should not run from pain. Pain is the body's way of letting us know that something might be off. It is there for a good reason.

Unfortunately, in some cases, it's unnecessary pain because we cause it within ourselves just because we are emotionally unhealthy.

Our beliefs, feelings and thoughts can heal us faster, make us sicker, cause us pain or keep us healthy.

In an article published in The New England Journal of Medicine in 2002, Dr. Bruce Moseley conducted a study on knee surgery for people with osteoarthritis.

He divided 180 patients into three groups: the first group, Moseley shaved the damaged cartilage in the knee. For the second group, he flushed out the knee joint, removing material thought to be causing the pain.

The third group was placed under anesthesia, but no surgery was performed. The patient was led to believe that they were receiving important surgery that would better their condition. After several minutes of pretending to perform surgery, Moseley and his assisting surgeons closed the small incisions they had made and released the patients.

All three groups received the same post-operative care and exercise programs. The group who had received no surgery, experienced the same levels of success as the groups who had the real surgery.

Moseley said, "My skill as a surgeon had no benefit on these patients. The entire benefit of surgery for osteoarthritis of the knee was the placebo effect."

One of the patients from group three, who had walked with a cane before, was even seen to be walking and playing basketball after his "pretend-surgery."

The placebo effect is where the doctor prescribes a sugar pill to the patient without the patient's knowledge. No actual medicine is prescribed. In many of those cases, the patient became well after taking the placebo pill.

There have been countless studies done about how much a person's beliefs and feelings affect the procedure, cure and recovery process.

Unfortunately, this is true for the negative aspect as well as the positive. Misdiagnosis can be fatal to the patient who believes that they may be dying. There have been recorded cases where a patient has died of a fatal disease but autopsy results showed that there was no fatal disease.

I once read about a physician who had misdiagnosed a patient with cancer. He had said, "I thought he had cancer. He thought he had cancer. Everybody around him thought he had cancer... did I remove hope in some way?"

In fact, patients with cancer move through the recovery process faster if they generally feel positive, laugh often and are surrounded by the love and support of family and friends.

This does not mean that we should refuse appropriate medication or surgery and just feel good all the time. It just means that our emotional and mental response with medication and surgery can make the difference between being healthy and becoming sick again.

Happy people have a healthier immune system and are less likely to become sick. This doesn't mean that happy people don't get cancer or become ill. It just means that the chances are a lot less because happy people have a healthier immune system.

Angry, stressed and depressed people have a low resistance to illness and can become sick faster or more often. Not to mention the fact that all of these things can cause high blood pressure, diabetes, thyroid problems and many other illnesses that can keep us sick.

In the 1940s, students at Harvard University participated in a study on the correlation between a person's mental health and their physical health. Based on their personal, reflective essays, students were classified as pessimists or optimists. Their health history was examined 30 years later.

Pessimists had a more serious range of diseases and health problems than their optimistic counterparts.

There are many studies on this topic, suggesting that negative mental health can create negative physical health.

In the words of Jim Rohm: "Take care of your body. It's the only place you have to live."

It's important to get regular exercise and eat healthy. However, if your emotional and mental state is negative, stressful and unhealthy, it won't be long until you begin to see the effects in your body.

QUOTE:

"If the mind, that masters the body, ever forgets and tramples on its slave, the slave is never generous enough to forgive the injury, but will rise and smite the oppressor." -Henry Wadsworth Longfellow

"Breaking the Cycle"

"Man is the only kind of varmint that sets his own trap, baits it, then steps in it." -John Steinbeck, Sweet Thursday

I first learned about Émile Coué's The Law of Reversed Effort or The Reverse Law, as I like to call it, when I was in my late teens. There was no real sense in The Reverse Law but it made life make sense.

The Reverse Law is very simple; when you try to stay on the surface of the water, you sink and when you try to sink, you float. If you catch your breath, you lose it.

This law is simple; we are likely to get back the opposite of what we put effort into. Another way of saying it is, the more we work toward "not" getting something, the more likely it is that we will end up getting it.

We have a tendency to focus on what we don't want instead of what we want. Have you ever tried very hard to avoid something and ended up walking right into it? For instance, you drive carefully so you don't get a ticket and your mind is so focused on not getting a ticket that you miss a stop sign and get a ticket.

You try very hard to be quiet in a room with a sleeping relative and you end up knocking something over or spilling something when you try not to spill.

So how does The Reverse Law work?

Say I want to lose weight. Instead of focusing my efforts on exercising and eating healthy (creative), I focus on avoiding certain foods and avoiding temptation (avoidance). That is why it doesn't work.

When people try to quit something, they don't place that energy into something creative or productive, they place that effort on avoiding cigarettes and avoiding the temptation to smoke.

We have a tendency to focus more on what we don't want than on what we do want.

Avoidance doesn't work. How can you show avoidance? If I were to show you my exercises and the healthy foods I just cooked for dinner, I would have something to show you regarding my plan to lose weight. It's tangible. You can see it, picture it, therefore I can produce results.

How can I show you avoidance? Can you see that? Can you picture that? Avoidance doesn't really exist. Avoidance is thinking. So how can you focus your effort on thinking? All it's going to do is make you do that which you don't want.

So when we work hard to try to accomplish something that doesn't really exist, we end up getting what we didn't want.

Since avoiding doesn't really exist, we're left only with the thing we didn't want.

"I'm avoiding cigarettes." "I am" is real. "Cigarettes" are real. However "avoiding" is not. So all we are left with is "I am" and "Cigarettes." Two things we can imagine very clearly, both together and apart.

What does that do to us psychologically? What is the conversation in my head every day? "I don't want cigarettes. I can't have cigarettes. No cigarettes. I'm stressed, I need a cigarette. No, I can't have cigarettes. Alright fine, maybe this one time."

The word cigarette repeats so many times during my Self-Talk that I end up causing actions that support my want: the cigarettes.

I will end up talking myself into having a cigarette because that is the only thing I'm focusing on.

Therefore, instead of avoidance, we must focus our attention on something creative that produces results in the place of the thing we don't want. The mind must be away from cigarettes, focusing on something else, not avoiding cigarettes.

There is a great saying, "What you resist, persists." In other words, the more you fight something, the stronger it becomes.

The human mind is designed to think of what it doesn't want and can't have. If I say, don't think of an elephant, I know that your mind just pictured an elephant. That is how we are. We cannot fight it. We must redirect it. There is no need to fight only to shift focus.

Imagine if I was an alien who had just come down to Earth and you were showing me things that humans do. You can show me what smoking looks like, you can show me what exercise looks like. Can you show me avoidance?

You can show me sitting. However, all I would see is you sitting, not you avoiding standing. I wouldn't interpret you sitting as you avoiding standing.

You know you're avoiding smoking because your intention behind your act is that you're avoiding smoking. However, all I can see is the act, not the intention behind it. Your intentions only exist within you. What exists in the real physical world is the act.

The most common occurrence of The Reverse Law is a very widespread episode in relationships. When we have childhood issues with abandonment, we have a tendency to be afraid that the people we love are going to leave us.

Then, when we enter into relationships, we act out of fear and try to avoid having the other person leave.

Here's how it works: Say a woman is in a relationship with a man she is afraid of losing. She wants to avoid losing him, avoid pain and avoid being abandoned.

Her continuous Self-Talk involves abandonment and pain. Even though it's not what she wants, her internal conversations revolve around it.

She tries to avoid any of it from happening, therefore, she calls him often, wants to know where he is, what he's doing, who he's with, and constantly does things she believes will make him happy.

She focuses all her attention on keeping him from leaving. He starts to feel smothered and trapped. He begins to think about leaving and starts pulling away. She notices his distance and disconnectedness and suddenly realizes that her fear might be coming true and that he's thinking about leaving.

So what does she do? She smothers him some more, thinking that if she gave him a lot of love and attention that he would want to stay. He interprets her actions as controlling and he leaves.

She has given life to her fear. By acting from a place of avoidance and focusing all her attention on doing things that will make him want to stay, she causes him to leave.

However, if she had focused her attention and efforts on herself and her fears of abandonment instead of projecting it outwardly to the other person, she would not have caused her fear to occur.

If she was not trying to keep him from leaving, she would have been less paranoid, less controlling, calmer and much easier to be around, thus making him feel more at ease and less likely to leave.

It doesn't matter if it's the man or the woman in the relationship that has insecurities, fears or issues. Either one can destroy relationships by creating the thing they fear the most.

Have you ever tried to avoid a fight and ended up causing one instead? You say something you wouldn't have normally said because you're avoiding an argument and what you said ends up upsetting the other person.

Avoidance causes us to act differently from how we normally would. I would have normally done this, but since I'm avoiding something, I'll do this instead. We act out of character and this shifts the world and people around us.

Due to The Reverse Law, we all fall into our own traps. We cause the things we don't want because we focus our attention and efforts on negative things.

In trying to be perfect, we mess everything up and create imperfection.

All efforts should be directed to tangible things that produce results. Focuses need to be shifted from what we don't want to what we do want.

Some things, however, can be disguised as wants when really they're only wants because we're still trying to avoid something else. For instance, you want a happy marriage. This may not seem like an avoidance, but the intention behind wanting a happy marriage might be because you want to avoid being alone, looking bad or admitting you failed.

Some parents encounter The Reverse Law issue when they have their child's best intentions in mind. They try to control their children to keep them safe and the child ends up acting out of control and careless thus creating the situations the parents are desperately trying to avoid.

Unfortunately, this just causes more problems for both. The parent wants to control the child's actions, wants and needs, and ends up causing distance between the two; something neither wanted nor set out to do.

Once you understand that The Reverse Law is at play, you can begin to understand how your actions affect the outcome. All it takes is a little shift. When you shift, the world shifts.

If we are not aware of The Reverse Law and its effects, we can get stuck committing the same mistakes repeatedly and receiving the results we didn't want.

We see this in life many times. People turn to religion to become peaceful; instead, they become angry, judgmental or violent. When governments try to force people to be moral by creating many prohibitions, people become criminals and revolt. When we create many weapons to keep ourselves safe, we become less secure.

The Reverse Law does not work when it comes to emotions, only effort. You can be afraid every day that your husband is going to leave, but that won't cause him to leave. It's when you act out of your fear that triggers The

Reverse Law. However, the more attention, focus and energy you place on a feeling the more you will feel of it because of the chemicals in your brain.

Effort, however, needs to be redirected into the appropriate place. When it comes to other people, instead of placing effort on changing things in other people that we don't like, we must turn our efforts inside.

When we try to change people because of our own insecurities or prejudices, it drives them away. People can become very defensive and upset if we point out their faults.

People tend to stop listening once the verbal attack starts. Remember that the voice is interpreting and getting more furious with every sentence.

They can't hear your judgment of them because the voice inside their head is far too busy being offended and coming up with a defense and an attack of its own.

We may think we're helping people by pointing out what they're doing wrong, but it only places a strain in our relationships.

People stop listening when we start criticizing, judging and blaming. It is not the way to change.

We must work on ourselves, not others. If we all looked inward, we wouldn't need to change others.

Instead of blaming someone else for their lack of attention to us, we should look within and work on our need for constant attention.

People you don't like can teach you many things about yourself. Anyone in your life who is a problem can teach you the most about yourself.

How you handle them and their problems says far more about yourself than it does of them.

We can't expect others to change and fit into our ideas of who they should be.

We tell ourselves that we try to change others because it would benefit them, when in reality we want them to change because it would benefit ourselves. We try to change others for our benefit knowingly or unknowingly.

When we struggle to change people, we have stress, anger, frustrations, war, murder and hatred all the time. All due to our need to change others (beliefs, ways, customs, thoughts, feelings, actions) to fit into our molds or ideas of who they should be.

We have to ask ourselves, where did we get this idea of how everyone should be? Why do you believe all people should be a certain way? Where does this belief come from?

We must ask important questions about our beliefs. Does this belief benefit you? Does it help your life? Is it needed? What is it needed for? Who originated this belief before you believed it?

What do you gain from this belief? What do you sacrifice in order to keep believing it? Most importantly, is the sacrifice worth it?

QUOTE:
"Human beings invent just as many ways to sabotage their lives as to improve them." -Mark Goulston, *Get Out of Your Own Way: Overcoming Self-Defeating Behavior*, 1996

CYCLES OF NEGATIVITY:
"A society does not simply discover its 'others,' it fabricates them, by selecting, isolating and emphasizing an aspect of

another people's life, and making it symbolize their difference." -William Green

If we want to look at cycles of negativity that hurt others, we must first be aware that they are more damaging to ourselves than they are to others. Some of these cycles include hate, discrimination, criticism and violence.

We usually see these things as being projected outside ourselves and therefore not about us. However, cycles of negativities are far more of a reflection of the individual projecting it than the person on whom it is being projected.

Hate is not a genetic trait that one is born with. Hate is taught. No one is born with a prejudice against a particular group. Parents, friends or anyone else with an influence in the child's life teaches the child hate.

We do a great disservice to our children when we teach them to hate or separate themselves from others just because of their differences. We set them up to believe that everything should be separated, which is the direct opposite of the nature of things.

Hate is like an internal poison within the body. There is no benefit for anyone involved. Imagine if you stored poison in your body for years just because of your own beliefs about someone else. Is your internal poison going to hurt the other person or you?

What does it benefit you to keep all of that poison inside? How does hating someone else help you?

You might say that you are just defending yourself and that your hate is only a result of another person's hate toward you.

So I ask you the question, what are you defending?

We develop an image of ourselves based on our upbringing. We are usually unconscious of this image until it becomes attacked. Suddenly, we go on the defensive and attack back.

You are not defending who you are. You are defending an image. Who you are doesn't require a defense because it cannot be attacked or harmed.

When you have no false image of self to feed and defend, hatred, greed, pride and arrogance disappear.

When you know who you are, other people's ridicule, criticism or hate can't hurt you.

When you truly see yourself and others as they truly are, you will see unity, not division.

Racism and prejudice are forms of self-hate. Most people think that racism comes from the racist's feelings of a superiority of race. As we already know, a superiority complex usually masks an inferiority complex.

When a teacher is a great teacher, he feels the need to share his wisdom. He encourages growth. It is only through sharing his wisdom that be becomes great.

If the teacher felt that he was the smartest and became threatened by a smart student and tried to kill him because of that threat, we would not say that the teacher was a great teacher.

So how can a great race ever try to wipe out other races because it was threatened by them?

A truly great race is beneficial to other races, especially to those that require a helping hand.

Is a police officer great because he kills other great police officers so that he can be the only great officer?

Is a great doctor one who teaches his methods to other doctors so that everyone can benefit or one who tries to destroy the advancement of other doctors because it makes him look bad?

We frown upon those types of negative behaviors and yet we do it to others.

What is it that we are defending? Are we defending races, religions and ourselves or are we defending the images we have created of ourselves?

No one can attack your religion. Your relationship with God is between you and God. No one can interfere with that. No one can enter your mind and heart and stop you from believing in or loving God.

Is it our religion we are trying to defend or our egos and prides? Is it an image or the self we are defending?

If you can justify the discrimination you feel toward others, just remember that others can justify discrimination toward you.

"Do unto others as you'd have done to you." People really don't want to be discriminated against. So why do we do it to others?

There is no one group of people that have been free from discrimination.

The Jews, Armenians, Palestinians, Americans, Turks, Muslims, Indians; we have all lost people because of where we were born. We have all fought each other trying to defend our images and egos. But who are we fighting?

No group who has been persecuted and discriminated against should ever turn around and do the same to another group.

If we only mourn for our own people's tragedies then what will stop us from doing the same to others?

One particular group cannot hold the monopoly on wisdom and virtue. Each culture has a unique gift to offer humanity. We all can learn from each other and grow as a whole.

If you can justify all the reasons why a certain group is wrong, disgusting, bad or evil, just know that there is another group out in the world who can say the same about you. Does it make it true?

The problem lies in our language. We look at "others" and see them as "others." There is no "we" only "us vs. them." When we live in an "us vs. them" world, we never run out of people we can make enemies of.

Remember that it is our innate ability to categorize and simplify that aids discrimination. It doesn't make it true.

No two people are the same. There may be similarities but no two people can ever be the same. Just like situations can't be the same. There can be similar situations but never the same. We judge them as the same because we only focus on the things that are similar.

The voice inside your head vocalizes these judgments. Consider it a judging machine that never stops.

When we later encounter something or someone similar, we automatically judge. No additional information is required.

Sometimes we keep our negativity to ourselves, allowing it to eat at us, and other times, we project them onto others.

Some people turn to violence and other people use mental or emotional abuse.

Constant criticism and verbal attacks can do just as much damage, if not more, to the human psyche than violence can.

A psychology professor once told me that criticism is more of a reflection of the critic's self-criticism than an assessment of the receiver.

Criticism says more about the critic than the person who is receiving it. Sometimes people criticize other people for the characteristics they hate within themselves.

I used to have a boss who felt the need to always micromanage. I used to take it personally, thinking that she believed I was incompetent. Later, I realized that it wasn't about me; it was about her. Her life was in shambles and she needed something to control to make herself feel better. She needed to grip onto something, so she paid too much attention to detail and felt the need to control everything. She was overwhelmed with insecurity and could only feel secure if she controlled things.

She didn't realize that her constant criticism, negativity and controlling behavior was making her employees resentful, frustrated and rebellious.

Would you rather be around someone who listens to you and appreciates you or someone who criticizes you and puts you down?

One of the most in-depth management studies ever conducted (The Carrot Principle, Chester Elton and Adrian Gostick, 2007, The Free Press) followed 200,000 people over ten years.

It found dramatically greater business results when managers offered helpful praise and meaningful rewards in ways that powerfully motivated employees to excel.

The study found that the main important characteristic of the most successful managers was that they provided their employees with frequent and effective recognition.

Employee appreciation and recognition is the driving force of successful companies like Pepsi Bottling Group, DHL and Disney, who were all a part of the study.

Appreciation inspires generosity, hard work and it inspires the person being appreciated to return the appreciation.

Criticism inspires resentment, anger, low self-esteem and possibly violence.

Criticism is a form of negative reinforcement. If we use negative reinforcement, it leaves the person confused. Now I know I'm not supposed to do this because I got hit, but what's the correct behavior? With positive reinforcement and appreciation, it's clear what the correct behavior is and if it is repeated, it is rewarded.

In my culture, the Armenian culture, children are expected to behave a certain way, and they are not appreciated for it because it is expected. When the expectations are not met, they receive negative reinforcement, i.e. criticism.

If a child gets good grades, it is not appreciated because that is what the child is supposed to do. They are supposed to get good grades and receive a diploma. And when they don't, they get verbally abused, criticized or punished. They are made to feel guilty and they are told that they have shamed the family reputation. The parents' egos take priority over the child's wellbeing.

That is negative reinforcement. It leaves the person with low self-esteem, feelings of inadequacy and repressed rage. All of those things can build up within the individual and they might become verbally abusive or violent toward their own family, strangers or spouses. It damages the person and a new cycle is created.

We react through the insecurities, frustrations and self-hate we have learned. Our reactions cause negative reactions in others and we feel justified in hating them, criticizing them or physically hurting them. We feed the cycle and keep it going. Not only do we suffer in the process but others do as well.

Years ago, I heard a man speak about a hate crime that he had committed. He had beaten a black man just because he was black. He spent five years in prison for committing that hate crime.

He spoke about his one-year-old son who did not see his father for the first few years of his life.

He said the worst thing about what he had done was having to face his six-year-old son who did not remember him. He said, "What do I tell my son when he asks, 'Dad why did you miss five years of my childhood? Where were you when I learned how to ride a bike or swim?'"

Ultimately, he had realized that his actions spoke louder than any words or excuses he could offer his son. His actions said that his hate for the stranger he beat up was far more important than the love for his own son.

He said, "I treated him like trash. I hurt him to take his power away but I took my own power. I took my freedom and five years of my life. And for what?"

If he had treated the stranger as his equal, they would have been equals. However, since he treated him as someone who was lower than he was, it was he who became lower than the stranger.

Martin Luther King Jr. said, "Let no man pull you low enough to hate him."

His hate didn't just cost him five years of his life, but also five years of his son's time with his father, his wife's time with her husband and his mother's time with her son. He took away from his family, friends and those he loved because his hate was more important than his family.

We lose so much when we hate, discriminate or use violence against others. Ultimately, we are the losers in those situations. We certainly aren't winners. What could we possibly win?

We lose relationships, our health, happiness and we take those things away from others. What's our gain?

People who are different from us should be cherished. How can we grow if we only hear things we've always heard or surround ourselves with people who think like us?

It's important to hear all sides, opinions and thoughts. You don't have to agree with what is being said, you just need to listen. It's not about agreement; it's about growth.

Some people listen from a place of finding faults. The only thing their filter picks up is what they don't agree with. They don't review the information or think longer about it. It's automatically shut out.

It's kind of like having certain letters of the alphabet. With ten letters, you can form only so many words. All you have to do is throw in one more letter and suddenly a multitude of opportunities for words arises.

People are like the letters of the alphabet, and when you connect with enough people, you have the world opened up to you and possibilities begin to pour in.

In the end, if we have an issue with someone, it's more of a reflection on us. If someone does something to bother me, I don't ask, why did they do that? I ask, why does it bother me?

After all, the person can do the same thing and other people might not be bothered by it, so why am I? It's important to look within and not throw blame out. If you're bothered by something, it's not the other person's fault. It's a reflection of you.

It seems like many things are a reflection of the self. Hate, discrimination, criticism, etc. Everything you project out comes from within. Sounds easy, of course; everything that is projected out has to come from within, where else can it come from?

If it's that easy, why are we projecting such negative things? Why are we actively making our lives miserable? Is it because we feel like we are victims and we have no control over the course of our lives? If that's the case, then what is the point of life? Why are we living if we are all just victims of everything else?

Cycles can be broken. Cycles of hate and violence can be broken through awareness.

It is only through awareness that we clean out our filters. When you can look at someone or something and see it as it is and not the label, then and only then can you truly see. The absence of judgment allows us to appreciate reality.

It's pretty remarkable that we have so many different people among us. What a wonderful opportunity to learn from each other and appreciate each other.

All of these different cultures and religions make the world beautiful. What if the world was filled with just roses? The beauty of the rose would diminish. If there were no contrast, there would be no beauty.

Why do we fight so hard to make others similar to ourselves? Especially when we don't like ourselves most of the time.

If 80 percent of our thoughts are mainly negative thoughts about our lives or ourselves, then why do we fight so hard to make others think, believe or act as we do? Are they really better off being us?

Do we really want everyone in the world to think, feel and act just as we do? Would this make the world a "better" place?

We are all unique. Each individual is a distinctive piece of a large puzzle. Imagine if we were all the same piece. Nothing would ever come together and, in the same way, we are all connected.

QUOTE:
"In the end anti-black, anti-female, and all forms of discrimination are equivalent to the same thing – anti-humanism." -Shirley Chisholm

---

LOVE AND THE ABSENCE OF LOVE:
"There is more hunger for love and appreciation in this world than for bread." -Mother Teresa

So many times, we confuse attention, obsession, lust and abuse for love.

We develop false ideas of what love and marriage are and we attempt to control others to fit into our ideas.

Some people love as long as certain conditions are met. "I love you as long as you are skinny, healthy or attractive." "I love you as long as things are good."

Once the circumstances change, the love goes away. Love is unconditional. Unconditional love means just that. There are no conditions attached to love. There are no prerequisites to love.

You can never predict who it is that you will fall in love with. You can't predict their skin color, height, weight or anything else. You may have some preferences but ultimately, you have no control over love.

Some people can't love because they lack the ability to give into it. Love requires a form of surrender. Some people can't surrender to love because they are too controlling or possessive. They feel powerless in life and fight to control everything and therefore can't truly love anything.

For some people marriage is more important than the person they are marrying.

Some girls I knew in school wanted to get married desperately. They didn't have a boyfriend or anyone in mind. They didn't care who it was, they just wanted to get married.

They had their own idea of what marriage was like and wanted it even though there was no one for them to marry.

Some people marry just to marry. They settle for people who come around because they're more in love with the idea of marriage than they are with the person they married.

They obsess over weddings, houses and rings, not realizing that marriage goes beyond those things. Marriage is not a ring, wedding date or property. Marriage is a relationship, not a commodity.

Marriage is just a fancier term for relationship. It is the relationship aspect of marriage that requires attention, love and energy.

When you marry someone, you must be prepared for the person to change in ways you never expected.

You are always growing and changing. Your spouse will grow and change.

Other people's changes are not on your schedule. Everyone around you will change. Everyone around you is changing at this moment in time. Some may grow with you. Some may grow apart from you.

You don't know who your partner will be one year, five years or ten years from now. Most importantly, you don't know who you will be five years from now. Your changes might not be as obvious to you as they may be for others around you.

Whether the relationship is between a parent and a child or a married couple, all parties involved must be aware that unforeseen changes are a part of the relationship.

Who is it that you love? Do you love the person as they are or an image or idea of the person you made up in your mind?

What happens when the person acts differently from the image we created? We get upset and fight with them. We try to change them or we leave them.

How can we be sure that we love the person and not the image of the person or what we want the person to be? You can't love someone for their potential and hope that once you're married things will be different. Assume for a moment that the person will stay exactly as they are for the rest of your lives, do you still want to marry them? Or are you hoping things will change?

Things will in fact change. However, we can't enter into a relationship unhappily hoping that things will change. They might not change the way we had hoped.

If you enter into a relationship wanting the other person to fix you, guide you, help you, solve your problems or save you then you are setting yourself up for disappointment and suffering. The same applies if you enter into a relationship to fix the other person, guide them, help them, solve their problems or save them.

If there is a sense of "need" it sets up the relationship for disappointment because you are always looking to the other person to fill your needs.

You don't need someone else to make you feel whole. You are whole. You don't need someone else to help you solve your problems or make you feel better about yourself.

Those are symptoms of low self-esteem or no confidence. You can take care of yourself. If you rely on your partner for that, you will remain disappointed.

Assumption in a relationship leads to disappointment and suffering.

You can't assume that your partner knows what you are thinking, feeling or what you meant by what you said. In addition, you can't assume that you know what your partner is thinking, feeling or what they really meant by what they said.

When you build your communication grounded on reality and not on assumptions and expectations, you can begin to build a relationship that does not require much energy to maintain.

It becomes far simpler to exist in the relationship. Instead of spending hours wondering what they really meant by what they said, instead of arguing in circles for hours or days without either person talking about what is truly bothering them, you can spend a few minutes communicating truthfully and then move on.

There is one important rule to have in any relationship, whether it be romantic or platonic: No blame, no shame, no complain.

They are poison for your relationships. When we blame others for how we feel, we leave them feeling defensive, angry or shameful. When we shame others for saying, doing or feeling a certain way, we create resentment and anger. When we complain about how others feel, act or speak, we leave them shamed and defensive. It doesn't benefit the relationship. All it does is feed the cycle.

There are many things that we unknowingly do that work against the relationship we are trying to preserve.

Owing in a relationship leaves imbalance. Someone owes the other an apology, a favor, dinner, etc. No one owes you anything. Either you do things for other people out of love, or you don't do it. If you do it expecting something in return, you set yourself up to be disappointed or upset.

The Persian poet Hafiz illustrated this point beautifully when he said, "Even after all this time the sun never says to the earth 'you owe me.' Look what happens with a love like that, it lights the whole sky."

Many times in relationships, we tend to compare our relationship with other people's relationships. We also compare the person we are in a relationship with. The neighbor's son is getting straight A's, why can't you get straight A's? So-and-so's husband bought her a diamond ring because he loves her, what have you bought me?

Comparison leads to criticism of the relationship or the person. It can also build up resentment toward the partner or cause the partner to build up resentment toward the criticizer. This is very toxic for a relationship.

As mentioned in the section before, criticism can create a very negative cycle leaving the criticized person with low self-esteem and resentment.

All it means is that the criticizer is not satisfied with the other person's behavior or actions and is attempting to correct it by criticizing them or shaming them into changing.

This is a form of manipulation that does not benefit the relationship or the other person. Blaming someone, shaming someone or complaining about someone is not beneficial to any relationship. It is just another form of control.

The person does not fit into the image of them that we have created so we fight to change them. Instead of adjusting our image, we attempt to adjust the person.

It is not the other person's responsibility or burden that you have unrealistic romanticized images of how they should act. You must ask yourself, are you more in love with the idea of love than with the person? Are you more in love with the image you have created in your mind of your partner than who they really are?

Do you have a predefined idea of how your relationship should be? Did you enter into the relationship with a clear image of how your partner and future with your partner would look like?

The problem with that is your partner may have entered the relationship with their own images and ideas of how you and the relationship should be as well. This will only leave the both of you disappointed, frustrated and unhappy.

If your partner disappointed you, you must ask yourself who it was who decided they should have acted differently in the first place?

If the other person is not given the room to grow, learn or make mistakes and is constantly criticized, shamed and blamed, the relationship becomes a negative cycle in itself and is unhealthy for both parties.

People in these situations try to mimic the outward appearance of love because the image is far more important than love itself.

Unfortunately, this means that they never love, only pretend to love. They may not consciously know that they are pretending and may have convinced themselves that it is love.

If I decide I want to be an athlete, I can buy athletic gear, hang out at the gym, and tell people I'm an athlete, but I'm not an athlete until I have played a game. The game may be scary at times, I may possibly get injured, but I'm not an athlete until I have played.

Therefore, we have people who want love, but instead of diving in and surrendering, they mimic what they think people in love act like. Time and time again, they find themselves unhappy, unsatisfied and disappointed with their partners and their relationships.

They can become controlling, trying to steer their partner and relationship.

Love is not possessive or controlling; it isn't supposed to make you feel bad about yourself, nor does it give you permission to make someone else feel bad about themselves.

Love is also not an addiction. Some people feel like they can't live or breathe without the other person. That is not love.

Love leaves a carefree feeling, not a controlling, obsessive feeling. That is an addiction or an obsession.

Many times, we become addicted to people because they give us a feeling we love or because they help feed an image of ourselves we believe or want to keep up.

People become addicted and trapped in patterns. Sometimes we choose people who keep those cycles moving, not because we love them but because we are stuck recreating emotions and situations we have become addicted to.

In other situations, we want to be with certain people because we can't be with them. Our egos and pride are attacked and we become obsessed with being with the person.

In cases of addiction and possessiveness, the relationship can become violent instantly.

In cases of abuse, women often return to the abuser not because they love him but because they don't love themselves. They believe that no one else will love them because they don't love themselves. What they don't realize is that love doesn't hurt.

If they do leave, much like a drug addiction, they often relapse and go back to the abuser. Usually because they think they can change him or because he has changed on his own.

It takes several attempts before they actually leave. Others end up dead or in prison for having killed their abusers.

We are all responsible for our own actions. If you are angry, you will find reasons to be angry. Other things don't make you angry, you already are angry and other things just give you an excuse to be angry.

Some people think that anger is situational. That it only happens with some people or some situations. Everything you feel and experience is projected out through you. You are where it begins. The problem lies with you.

This is not a judgment of you or your character; this is an awakening. If you do not wake up to your negative cycles, you will remain trapped in them. You will continue to feel angry and project rage onto others because you really feel powerless in life.

Powerful people don't feel the need to display their power abusively. Powerless people show extreme displays of power to mask feelings of powerlessness.

True power is not having power over others but having power over ourselves. Strength is being able to admit that we feel weak. Just as freedom is not physical, it is internal.

Recognizing someone else's power does not diminish yours. It doesn't make you any less powerful. Power comes from within. It can't be gained with force or violence.

In fact, most force and violence is a result of someone feeling powerless inside.

Perhaps it comes from being unhappy or feeling unloved.

When we don't feel loved, love is substituted for food, drugs, alcohol, sex, violence, shopping and things.

We all hunger for love, especially children. This is why children who don't feel loved can grow to become chronic criticizers or abusers later in life. They lack the ability to love others as they are because they lack the ability to love themselves as they are.

A child who feels whole doesn't want many things. All wants for toys, clothes, presents and things are nothing but fillers for what they really need, which is to feel loved, heard and wanted.

When we are conscious of our actions, we will stop acting and speaking out of insecurities, low self-esteem and self-hate. Almost everything you do is personal. Even when you do something for someone else, it's really for you.

Criticizing, abusing, and becoming addicted to someone are all reflections of how we feel inside. Someone who criticizes others isn't happy with themselves. Someone who abuses others feels low about themselves. Someone who is addicted to someone else really wants to be loved completely; they believe that addiction is loving someone completely and wholehearted.

With love, the first thing we must do is rid ourselves of the images and ideas of how it is *supposed* to be or look like.

People in love hold hands, go out on dates, never argue, are jealous, have pet names for each other, have sex all the time, etc. Who decided all of this? Why do we believe it?

If we believe this notion that people in love must act a certain way then that means we all have to become different people just because we're in love.

The same can be said about the love between friends or family. There are images and ideas we all subconsciously believe about the people we love and how they *should* love us.

Love is acceptance. There are more pages on what love isn't than there is on what love is.

Love is accepting the other person for all that they are. Their faults, mistakes and idiosyncrasies are not judged as character flaws, criticized or shamed. They are allowed the freedom to grow and change. That is love.

QUOTE:
"There are four questions of value in life... What is sacred? Of what is the spirit made? What is worth living for, and what is worth dying for? The answer to each is the same. Only love." -Johnny Depp from the film *Don Juan deMarco*, 1995

KNOWING vs. BEING:
"Real knowledge is to know the extent of one's ignorance." - Confucius

Adam and Eve ate from The Tree of Knowledge of Good and Evil and they were thrown out of paradise.

When we fill our minds with good, bad, right and wrong, we can't know happiness, peace or paradise.

They were happy and peaceful with just being. Once knowledge filled their minds, they lost paradise.

When some things are good, that means that other things are bad. When some things are right then other things are wrong.

Social duality was introduced to their minds and paradise was lost.

Now we play the game of I'm right, you're wrong; I'm good, you're evil. However, the person I feel is bad and wrong might feel the same way about me.

The tree was not truth, the tree was knowledge. They were already living in truth and they were happy just being in oneness with everything. Once an outside factor, the snake, introduced the idea of duality into their minds, they couldn't resist. After all, if all of the other trees are good to eat from and one is bad, then duality is beginning to surface within the mind.

They wanted to know. They ate from The Tree of Knowledge and became filled with knowledge and suffering. Paradise of oneness was lost.

They moved from a being of oneness and unity with everything to one of judgment and separation.

All our lives we have been taught that knowledge is power. We hold high regard to education and educated people. Yet education does not guarantee happiness or that our lives will be better than they were before we became educated.

We hold knowledge in our minds and occasionally we apply it in our lives. However, that doesn't change our lives. Knowledge is good, but it doesn't move mountains.

The key is not "knowing" but "being." You are not a human knowing; you are a human being.

A teacher doesn't have to think about being a teacher, she just is. Of course, she has gained some knowledge in school and she passes her knowledge to her students but who she's being everyday is not a woman with a degree; it's a teacher.

Who you're being, at any given moment, is reflected in your environment. It's not that your environment magically changes, it's that your filter changes. You notice only the things that reflect who you're being at that given moment.

We all know people who only focus on the negative, give them any situation and they will still find a way to complain about something. It's annoying and frustrating for everyone else but they're not consciously doing it; they're on Autopilot.

It's not that everything around them is bad, it's that who they're being doesn't allow them to see the good things.

Who they're being is reflected around them, not the other way around. We react to things around us but those things reflect us. Again, it's not that your environment magically changes, it's that your filter changes.

You filter out the good and only see the bad.

The same information, the same matter, and the same energy are around all of us. Why are we all receiving such different information?

A teacher wakes up in the morning thinking about her class, she turns on the news and hears something interesting. Her first thought is that she should tell her students.

An athlete wakes up that same morning. He's thinking about the three-mile run that he usually runs every morning. He's thinking about his sneakers that may be wearing thin, he's wondering if it might rain or if his route will be crowded.

He turns on the news, hears the same piece of information that the teacher did, eats his breakfast and goes out for his run. The moment he steps out of the door, what he heard on the news is forgotten.

What's the difference between the two? The teacher's filter is set to catch useful information that may be interesting to her students. She listens for news stories to discuss in class: information on the state budget and her annual salary, good books that her students may enjoy, etc.

The athlete's filter is different. A mother's filter is different. Everything else that the filter does not pick up is forgotten. It feels as though it never happened.

Many women notice how much their lives change after they become parents. It's not just the physical addition of another person that changes their lives, it's their mentality that changes their lives.

When you shift, the world shifts. Not because the world actually shifted, but because how you view the world did.

If I believe that the world is full of good people who help each other, I would be able to find proof of it. If I believe that the world is full of angry and violent people, I would be able to find proof of it.

Atheists don't believe that proof is possible and therefore it's not. Scientists can explain everything using science and believers can explain everything using God.

You see what you're looking for. You can find proof of any belief. "Seek and ye shall find."

You can even say, "But I know it's true. I have proof." So do I. What is knowledge anyway?

What we must keep in mind is that we're making decisions every single minute of every day with partial knowledge.

You decide your boss hates you. You decide you're stupid. You decide you can't do anything right. You decide to leave your house fifteen minutes before eight o' clock, fully knowing that there is traffic every morning.

We make decisions based on what we observe. Our observations then become our truths. If I view my boss's acts as negative toward me then I can conclude that my boss hates me. However, does that make it true?

For instance, when someone cuts you off in traffic, are they doing it to you or are they just doing it? If you had been another car, wouldn't they do the same thing? Haven't they done the same thing before and will they not continue to do the same thing, with or without you? Does that make the act personal?

How many of your everyday actions are actually personal against someone else? If 90 percent of behavior is habitual then how can it possibly be personal? A person acts the way they act because that is the way they act. If you were someone else, they would act the same way. It's not personal.

If everyone is carrying around internal negative beliefs about themselves, thinking negative thoughts and having negative Self-Talks, then most of the time their actions are about themselves, not you.

We must remember that we decide much of what we believe to be truth and most of what we decide is based on partial knowledge.

The significant difference between knowing and being is that knowing doesn't always reflect in your environment, being does.

We all know that if you drink and drive, your ability becomes so significantly impaired that you can crash the car and kill yourself or someone else. But does that stop us from doing it? Do people who drink and drive not know this information?

Do overweight people who eat large portions of unhealthy food not know that the food is unhealthy? Or is it that they know but do it anyway?

If I'm a smart kid living in a poor and dangerous neighborhood, my knowledge isn't going to save me from theft, assault or death. However, who I'm being will.

Even if I was smarter than the rest in my neighborhood but I was being negative, arrogant, and pessimistic, my intellect would not save my life or keep me from danger.

Being a teacher effects the environment, knowing things that teachers know, does nothing.

I can possess all the knowledge in the world, but if who I'm being is someone who is stressed, angry, pessimistic, anti-social and doesn't listen to anyone, how will my knowledge help me?

Who you're being at any given moment is the difference between happiness and unhappiness, between success and failure.

Knowing is half as powerful and effective as being. I've known people who were very bouncy and funny but less intelligent than most and yet they have gained a lot of success and progressed in their jobs because they are being fun, friendly and approachable people.

We are all complete. There is no emptiness within us. As soon as space opens up, it is automatically filled. When you get rid of an old belief, a new one takes it place. When you get rid of an old habit, a new one takes its place.

Since we are all filled inside, we can't add anything to what we already have. We must first make space by dumping out the old.

You already have thoughts, beliefs and feelings about everything. If I asked about "money," you can give me your thoughts, feelings and beliefs about money. Even if you don't currently have money. "I'm broke. I don't have any money." "It's hard making money." "It takes money to make money." All of these things contribute to who you're being.

Your money section is full. It will always be full. It's just a matter of what you fill it with. We believe that being isn't connected with money or relationships. We think that it's a matter of circumstance. "I just haven't found the right person." "I just don't have the right job or opportunities to make money."

If you are not willing to give up being a complainer, a pessimist or quick tempered you may miss those opportunities because you are too busy complaining, too busy judging people who might offer you opportunities, or pushing people and connections away.

Who is going to give you an opportunity if you don't meet them half way? Who is going to offer you a chance to become rich if you are negative, angry or can't communicate? Would you choose a business partner who is stubborn, aggressive and wants to do everything their way or someone who is willing to listen to you and your ideas, appreciates your contribution to the business and approaches everything with a calm, logical mind?

Would you rather buy from a company that appreciates your business, offers you a friendly smile and treats you like a human being or from a company that doesn't greet you, offers bad customer service and thinks that it's the one doing you a favor so you shouldn't complain?

It is far easier to give to someone who is open, nice and friendly because it makes us feel as though they deserve it, rather than giving to someone who is grumpy, closed off or anti-social. Who would you rather do a favor for? Who would you rather give an opportunity to?

It is all about being. You are a human being, not a human doing or a human speaking. Everything is dependent on what you are being.

What would it matter if you spoke pleasantly all the time but who you were being was an arrogant, self-righteous, self-centered jerk?

A dog is not considered a good dog because he is a good barker and a man is not a good man because he is a good talker.

Being isn't just speaking or acting. Being involves your thinking, beliefs, actions, feelings, behavior and attitudes. It is everything combined. In other words, it's your whole being.

Being creates your environment and defines your world.

If you decide that you will start thinking positively now and expect your whole world to change, you'll be disappointed. Altering one does not necessarily alter all.

Only by being aware of all of these factors can we begin to alter each one of them consciously.

You must be willing to give up old ways of being that aren't working for you and try a different approach.

How is it that you have handled your money so far? Perhaps it's not wise for you to have money with your current state of being. You're not rich now and that may be for a good reason. Perhaps you, as you are now, are not ready for that kind of responsibility.

If I say I want to be rich, is that the same thing as I am willing to be rich? Am I ready to give up being anti-social? Am I willing to give up being lazy? Am I willing to give up aggression? Being rich may require me to believe other beliefs, think other thoughts and behave differently. Am I willing to give up my old way of being?

I've known people who have had large sums of money come into their lives and within a month or so, it's gone. There it was, an opportunity to multiply that money. However, because of their way of being, it was gone again. They handled the money the way they always handle money and therefore it was gone. Some people are given $10,000 and turn it into $100,000, others are given the same amount and it's gone within a few weeks. But is it not the same opportunity?

You might say I want to find the right spouse. Are you willing to give up being selfish? Are you willing to give up not listening or being stubborn or not compromising? The right partner requires a different way of being. Are you willing to give up the old?

That's really the question here: Are you willing to give up your world? Because what you really want might not fit into your old world.

Perhaps there's no room in your world for wealth or another person.

You must first let go of your old ways of being in order to create the space for a new way of being. Only in giving up and letting go can we create the space required for the type of being that can radically alter our world.

QUOTE:
“How does one become a butterfly?" she asked. "You must want to fly so much that you are willing to give up being a caterpillar.” - Trina Paulus, *Hope For The Flowers*, 1997

WAITING FOR CHANGE:
"Some believe there is nothing one man or one woman can do against the enormous array of the world's ills - against misery, against ignorance, or injustice and violence. Yet many of the world's great movements, of thought and action, have flowed from the work of a single man. A young monk began the Protestant reformation, a young general extended an empire from Macedonia to the borders of the earth, and a young woman reclaimed the territory of France. It was a young Italian explorer who discovered the New World, and 32-year-old Thomas Jefferson who proclaimed that all men are created equal. ‘Give me a place to stand,' said Archimedes, ‘and I will move the world.' These men moved the world, and so can we all."- Robert F. Kennedy

One person can in fact make a difference. Nelson Mandela, Mother Teresa, Dr. Martin Luther King Jr., Mahatma Gandhi, Dalai Lama, Abraham Lincoln, Buckminster Fuller, etc.

They never waited for someone else to come by and change their worlds.

These are all great people who have changed our world by changing their worlds. They were not great because they were born great. They didn't have genes of greatness nor did they go to school for the great.

They were not great because they fought and didn't allow others to stop them. They were great because they didn't stop themselves.

You are your biggest enemy. You cause all the problems in your life. You cause your own suffering; you cause your own pitfalls. You stop yourself.

Your thoughts, beliefs, feelings and actions are your own. If you choose to not believe that you can achieve greatness, who is to be blamed for that?

Even if someone had told you that you couldn't achieve big, it was you who chose to believe it. People always have a tendency to ridicule, criticize and fight against great people. There is no one person who has been embraced by all.

People will tell you many things in life. It is your responsibility to figure out what you choose to believe and what you toss aside.

There are great people in the world, inspired and willing to help. In a small planet of six billion people, you are not alone. You will never be alone.

We all experience failure, but the difference between successful people and people considered failures is that successful people don't identify with their failures. They see them as stepping-stones to success instead of the end of the line.

What's the difference between them and you? Are they smarter than you? Do they have more money than you? Do they have more opportunity than you?

Those are just excuses we tell ourselves to make ourselves feel better about not trying or failing. Were there not others who were smarter than those people, richer or with more opportunity? Yet they didn't allow that kind of thinking to stop them. To someone else, you are smarter, richer and with more opportunity.

Greatness is not a destination. It is a process that never ends. If you stop the process, you stop being great.

Athletes don't stop practicing when they become great. They become great because they never stop practicing.

It begins with us. We are responsible for our greatness, weakness, success, and failure.

Sometimes people experience "bad" things after they decide to change their lives for the better. What they don't realize is that the "thing" isn't bad. Their interpretation of the thing is bad because they still think the way they used to think.

People believe that illness, losing jobs and accidents are "bad" things. There are no bad things - only things.

Think of it this way: If 90 percent of behavior is habitual and most people are on Autopilot, doing and redoing the same things, then how is your life going to change?

Where you are now and everything that you currently have or don't have is a result of all your previous thoughts, beliefs and actions. If you continue your previous thoughts, beliefs and actions then you will continue to receive more of the same.

Most of us continue thinking, believing and acting in the same manner but expect different results.

You can't wait for circumstances to change. You must change, and then the circumstances will change.

If you continue to think, believe and act in the same manner, you will create cycles by recreating your past over and over again.

Every moment is an opportunity for violence, for understanding, for compassion, for hate, for love… which opportunity you take is dependent on who you're being at that moment.

We cannot wait for others to change. We cannot wait for others to change our lives for us. We must make the first move if we want to be happy.

If we constantly focus on how different we want or wish our future to be, we will never change our present.

We focus on the future as a coping mechanism to help get through our present circumstances.

We're waiting for someone or something to come by and change our present. That's not powerful. That's more of victim thinking. It's passive action. It's waiting to react.

You can't wait for life to happen while you prepare yourself. You can't get a degree in life. Life is on-the-job training. We learn as we go. Life is always happening, whether we live it consciously or not. In the words of John Lennon, "Life is what happens to you when you're busy making other plans."

Many times, we become stuck on changing things. We feel that if we changed our job, our spouse, our income or our appearance that we would be happy.

If you have a problem here, you will have the problem somewhere else, because the problem lies with you. If people here make you angry, people somewhere else will make you angry too. You are angry. It's not the people who make you angry, it's you. Others cannot make you something else. It is your choice, responsibility and it is within your power.

It's not the things in our lives that need change, it's who we're being in the process of life. What would it matter if you suddenly won millions of dollars, but you became a paranoid, anxious, cruel person who didn't keep friends or talk to anyone? How would that money benefit you or anyone else?

Therefore, it is not the things in our lives that need changing; it is our perception of those things.

We can't wait around for others to change themselves or their behaviors to make us happy. They're usually busy trying to change others to make themselves happy.

You must change first. When you shift, the world shifts. Gandhi said, "Be the change you want to see in the world." Compassion and understanding are where it begins.

We must understand that we all have the same voice fueled by our own insecurities talking non-stop in our heads. We all come from different places of suffering when we perform simple actions.

We must understand, we can change the world - not by force, not by violence, not by religious dogma, but by simply changing our being.

QUOTE:
"The significant problems we face cannot be solved by the same level of thinking that created them."
-Albert Einstein

RIGHT NOW:
"The present is never our goal: the future alone is our goal. Thus, we never live but we hope to live; and always

hoping to be happy, it is inevitable that we will never be so." -Blaise Pascal

I've always been fascinated with people who can't sit still. As a child and as an adult I have had the ability to sit quietly for long hours. I rarely ever feel rushed, complain about long lines in grocery stores or feel bored. Even as a child, I entertained myself and never felt bored.

Every single member of my family is the exact opposite. I used to wonder why it was that they couldn't just "be." They always had to "do," but they found it difficult to just "be."

I can sit for hours without actively doing anything. Existing doesn't bother me. My family members on the other hand always feel the need to do something. There's always somewhere else they need to be.

My mother used to complain about long lines in the grocery store, about the slowness of the clerk at the register, about the slow drivers on the way home and once we would rush home there would be nothing urgent to do.

I believe it comes from a feeling of doing menial tasks. There are certain things we do in our everyday lives that seem unimportant, almost as if the task doesn't deserve our time or energy.

Let's face it, life is filled with tasks we don't want to do but sometimes must do; showering, buying groceries, brushing our teeth, driving to and from work, etc. However, when we add up all of these tasks, they take up a large majority of our time. Even if we rush them, we can't escape them. There will always be tasks to be done that we don't necessarily want to do.

Does that mean we should rush through them quickly, get angry, upset and frustrated? Is it wise to destroy our health for a few extra minutes? After all, if we were calmer and more peaceful instead of stressed and angry, we would be healthier. What are we collecting all those extra minutes for? What do we do with those extra minutes we "saved" by rushing? We use those extra minutes to think about other places we would rather be and other things we would rather do.

I believe that if, for whatever reason, I am somewhere, then that is where I am supposed to be for that moment in time. There is no "other" place I "should" be.

I choose not to spend a large majority of my day feeling as if I should be somewhere else. That only means that I'm never really anywhere.

Since there is no start and end point to the universe or to Earth, where you are is the center. Anywhere you move is the center.

Where you are is where you should be. If you are in the grocery store, that is where you should be. If you are at home, that is where you should be.

My former co-workers used to say that they couldn't wait to get home. Then they would tell me about how when they were home they spoke about what they did at work that day or what they would do at work the next day.

What would be the point of being anywhere if the mind is always thinking about somewhere else that it should be? When does it end? Even at night, there is no rest because the mind spends time on where it should be tomorrow.

Life is spent living in the future or past instead of now. It's always about what's next instead of what's now. This goes beyond menial tasks or grocery lines. Eventually, it leads to not living at all.

When we live in the future, we don't really live, we only hope to live. We want to live, but we never actually live because even when tomorrow becomes today our minds are still on tomorrow.

The present moment is all there ever is to experience life directly. The power lies in the now, not in then or in later.

Anywhere you go, you take right now with you. You can't lose right now. It's not back home or at a friend's house; it is always with you.

Right now is eternity because right now never ends. You can never step away from right now.

Just as there is no other time than now, there is no other place than here. Wherever you go, you are here. Even when you walk over there, it becomes here. You can never go "there."

We can't dwell in the past or escape into the future; we have to concentrate on the present moment. It is in the present moment where we hold the power. Tomorrow is an illusion in the mind.

Our minds carry the past and paint the future but they can only be used now. We cannot dwell in them nor allow them to take over our minds in constant thinking loops.

Suffering over your past or obsessing over your future will not make your present any better.

The only reason there is a past is because we remember it. The only reason there is a future is because we create it in our minds. In reality, the only thing that exists is the present.

You are aware in the present, not in the past or the future. Most importantly, you are aware that you are aware. It is through this awareness that you gain insight, power and freedom. “I think, therefore I am” becomes “I am aware that I think, therefore I am.”

Awareness is the ultimate power. When you are aware, you are free to choose in this moment.

This is the only moment you can ever have and when you are aware of that, you are powerful.

QUOTE:

“You must live in the present, find your eternity in each moment. Fools stand on their island opportunities and look toward another land. There is no other land, there is no other life but this.” -Henry David Thoreau

"The Real Truth"

"As long as people believe in absurdities they will continue to commit atrocities." -Voltaire

We perceive the world through our memories of the past, our dreams for the future and our perception of now; also known as our filter. We will always experience the world through our filter.

What we believe to be truth today might not be truth tomorrow. Every day we learn new information that changes the old information we held to be true. Does that make the information we have now false?

Science makes continuous discoveries that dramatically alter our beliefs about our world and our universe.

How much of what we know and believe can we trust? Science and religion have collective filters. It is a filter that has been agreed upon by a large group of people. That makes the information much more difficult to challenge because everything makes sense within its world.

How much of our perception of reality is actual reality? What is actual reality and does it exist outside ourselves?

The world we experience can only be experienced through our five senses: touch, smell, taste, sight and hearing.

Each one of these senses transmits information to the brain where it is interpreted. Everything you have ever known or experienced is an interpretation by the brain of information received through your senses.

So how do we know that what we touch, smell, taste, see or hear is true?

Our senses lie to us. If we place half of a long stick in water and leave the other half out of the water, it appears to the eye that the straight stick is bent in the water. If we look down railroad tracks, it appears to the eye that the tracks meet at the end, forming a tip.

There are things we see that are illusions to our eyes and then there are things that we can't see with our eyes. There are noises we hear and noises we don't hear.

There are vibrations so low that our ears cannot interpret them as sound. There are things that exist around us that we cannot see, touch, smell, hear or feel.

If our senses can't always be trusted to give us accurate readings about our environments, then how can we know reality?

Sound is a vibration floating and traveling through the air. It doesn't become sound until it reaches the ear drum. So then does sound exist if we're not there to hear it? If an eardrum is not present to pick up the vibration and convert it to sound, does sound exist in a reality where we don't?

If we relook at sound from this perspective then we can do so with other things we perceive.

Is my sweater blue or is it blue because I see it? Does color exist in reality? Does color exist outside of my mind?

Our senses transfer information to our brain, which then interpret things based on what it already understands.

What are things really like? What does blue really look like?

The grass registers as green to most human eyes. Is the grass green to someone who is colorblind? What is green and how do we know that we all see green the same way?

Due to the nature of the way humans are designed, we lack the ability to view or experience reality as it is. Instead, we each create our own reality.

Our perception (beliefs, opinions, memories, experiences) alters reality into a personal version of reality, which, in the end, corrupts the way we perceive the truth.

The real truth is experienced through our filters, senses and past experiences. Reality is diluted into our own version of reality.

When we look at something with a predefined idea about it, we tend to take those predefined ideas and see them whether they are there or not, thus making up our own truth.

If you believe that your mother hates you, regardless of what she does, you will only see actions that you can interpret as hate. Regardless of the intentions behind the actions, your interpretation is the same.

This problem comes from the fact that all information we receive is interpreted as personal because it must fit into our personal reality.

If mom arrived home upset at her boss and yelled about the dishes in the sink, that information will be interpreted as personal. To you, it has nothing to do with the boss or the job or even the dishes. It is perceived as a personal attack on you.

Reality may be that your mother is upset at someone else, but your filter only picks up the fact that she is yelling and interprets that as a wide variety of negative information: Your mom hates you, she thinks you're not good enough, she doesn't appreciate the work you do around the house, she doesn't care about your feelings, etc.

We cannot understand new information without the natural prejudice of our previous knowledge.

When actual objects are viewed without understanding, the mind will try to reach for something that it already recognizes, in order to process what it is viewing.

In other words, we can't experience something new without some comparison to the past. The new thing, itself, can't be experienced without our filters.

This is why we always use references we already understand to explain new things. If we were to stumble onto something completely new, we would immediately begin comparing it to something we already know.

It is round like a tennis ball, as red as blood, feels like rubber, it makes a sound like a quacking duck and it smells like barbecue.

Now, I'm not sure if something like that actually exists, but I have now described it in a way where if you come across it, you know what it looks like, what it feels like, what it smells like and what it sounds like.

You have just imagined this thing in your mind even though you never saw it, smelled it, touched it or heard it. So even though it doesn't exist, you would know it if you saw it, smelled it, touched it and heard it.

Since the human brain is designed to compare, nothing can be experienced for what it truly is. Whether it is the sun (which is a star, which is a ball of fire, which is an element in the universe) or the fire burning in a fireplace. They are different entities but also the same.

They are the same in the sense that they all belong to the universe. They are different in the way we relate to them.

Our labels for things confuse our perception, behavior and relation to them.

There's a story about a teacher who picks up a hand fan and asks his students what the fan's purpose is. One student picks it up and fans himself. The second student picks it up, puts a slice of cake on it, and serves the teacher some cake. The teacher then smiles at the second student acknowledging that the second student understood the lesson.

If we only see things with the purpose we give them, we lose possibilities and diminish purpose. Moreover, if we define the new thing with properties of the thing we know, we misunderstand the new thing and its possible uses.

We believe that resourceful people are highly intelligent people because they can make use of anything around them. Ultimately, all they are doing is not limiting things to our basic ideas of what they should be. They can see outside of labels.

We all create distinctions in our minds. It aids us in understanding our world and universe.

There is no East or West. Humans created the distinction East and West to help ourselves navigate. We created time, days, weeks, months, years, decades and centuries. It helps us categorize events that we can neatly file away in our minds or on paper.

We created the constellations. There is no constellation Aries or Gemini, they are just stars. We have chosen to draw lines through stars and give them names. This helps us map the sky.

We are surrounded by distinctions created by the human mind. Sometimes we forget that we made them up. Who decided that a hand fan should only be used as a hand fan and cannot be used to serve cake?

Our view of the outside world is full of symbols, images, words, numbers, inches, meters, miles, pounds and other things we have invented.

Longitude, latitude, weights, measurements, distances, math, language and symbols are all in the mind.

How much of the world we "know" is made up? How much of the world do you actually see?

We have stopped viewing our world the way it is and only see our made up distinctions.

Is there an actual reality or is reality only what we interpret and see? Is there anything that exists outside of our filter, and can we ever know or experience it?

The mind creates much of the world around us and we forget or are not aware that it does, accepting everything we see and experience as fact.

Ultimately, the outside world exists inside ourselves. We have created it and it only exists because we do.

The outside world is internalized and the internal world is projected out. Outside blends into inside and inside flows out. If this relationship is in harmony and balance, there is peace.

The problem is that we try to change the out to match the in. When the only thing we can change is the in. We struggle, force and fight the outside world to fit into our internal world.

We can harmonize with the outside world through awareness of our judgments, prejudices and beliefs toward it.

What is your source for the information you receive regarding the outside world? It's either the voice in your head, or the voice from someone else's head.

How can we trust the information we receive when the source is not designed in our favor?

We all make statements like, "It's a bad day." But is it? Are there actual bad days in reality?

There are no bad days, only days. You decide in your mind whether it is good or bad. But if that is truly the case, why do we choose so many bad days?

What we think, believe and feel makes up so much of what we experience and how we experience it.

Critics will always find something to criticize and optimists will always find something to be positive about. You can actively test this theory. Find something great and look for a fault. Then, find something you hate and look for the positive.

George W. Bush had the lowest approval rating of any president and yet he had followers who believed that he did a great job. Abraham Lincoln is considered America's greatest president and he had violent opposition; he was assassinated.

We are the creators of our lives and worlds. Why do we create such negative, toxic and unhealthy lives and worlds?

QUOTE:
"Everyone who enjoys thinks that the principal thing to the tree is the fruit, but in point of fact the principal thing to it is the seed. -- Herein lies the difference between them that create and them that enjoy." -Friedrich Nietzsche

---

THE TRUTH IS...:
"There are no facts, only interpretations." -Friedrich Nietzsche

The human brain is not like a computer. It doesn't just store a bunch of information as facts and recall them exactly.

The information is stored in the hippocampus of the brain, and then when we recall it, our brain reabsorbs the information and stores it again. This time, however, it is reprocessed. In other words, the same information that is reprocessed in the brain is slightly different from the first.

Over time, the information is transferred to the cerebral cortex and it becomes separated from the context in which it was originally learned.

For example, you probably know that the capital of France is Paris, but you most likely don't remember how or where you learned it.

This phenomenon, known as source amnesia, can also lead people to forget whether a statement is true. If you receive information that may not be true, over time, you might believe it to be true because you forget where you learned it.

Over the time it takes to transfer information from one part of the brain to the other, you forget the source of the information, and the message and its implications gain strength. Over time, this misremembering only gets worse.

I remember a friend I had in junior high who always told the same story differently each time. Every time she retold the story there was a fact or two that she added or subtracted until eventually the story turned into a different story.

Of course, it's now that I understand that she wasn't intentionally lying or exaggerating. It seems that when we tell a story, we form opinions and feelings about it and then when we retell it, we fuse our opinions with the story and retell it differently.

We tend to remember news that agrees with our worldview and ignore statements that contradict it. There have been studies done with university students regarding how much we allow our beliefs to affect the information we allow our brains to accept.

The Stanford University study with 48 students split the students in two groups, half of whom said they favored the death penalty and half of whom said they opposed it. They were presented with two pieces of evidence, one supporting and one contradicting the claim that the death penalty prevents crime.

Researchers discovered that both groups were more convinced by the evidence that already supported their initial beliefs.

Researchers also found that even when the students were specifically instructed to be objective, they were still prone to reject the evidence that disagreed with their beliefs.

Even when we try to be objective, we are still biased toward our own beliefs.

How do we usually know that something is fact? We rely on cause and effect to show us. For instance, if I place my hand on fire (cause), I will get burned (effect). Therefore, I can conclude that placing your hand on fire burns.

This innate ability has helped us survive for thousands of years. Through cause and effect, we learned that if a vicious animal attacks, we would die. If we don't have food, we would die. If we don't keep warm, we would die. In order to survive, we must eat, stay warm and keep away from danger.

It was important to have cause and effect when we were learning that hand on fire burned. Now we use cause and effect differently. We apply it to our social world, receive mixed results and the confusion causes anxiety.

We are very quick to make facts out of beliefs because of cause and effect. For instance, I dropped my plate and mom yelled at me, therefore mom hates me. I messed up (cause) mom hates me (effect).

We use our ability to find facts for our survival to our disadvantage. It seems as if cause and effect frequently reveals that we are limited, unintelligent, undeserving failures. Perhaps not all of those at the same time, but we have all felt that way at some point or another.

Our innate abilities that were once crucial to our survival currently get in the way of our communication and connection with each other.

It's important to have cause and effect when you need to know that if you stand in front of a speeding train, you will get hit.

It was important to have the ability to divide when we are dividing portion of food among our children.

It's important to have stress and anxiety when we need adrenalin to pump through our bodies and muscles in order for us to fight for our lives or escape from danger.

We live in populated societies and civilization but carry the same abilities that kept us alive thousands of years ago. Since we don't have the danger of the saber-toothed tiger, we have created saber-toothed tigers everywhere. The traffic, our bosses, our neighbors - it seems as if the enemy is everywhere. It seems as if danger and stress are everywhere.

We misuse cause and effect to our own personal disadvantage; we misuse the ability to divide by dividing everyone into simple categories. We misuse stress and anxiety by applying them in our everyday lives. If the line at the store is a little longer than we expected, we stress. If we are stuck in traffic, we stress. If someone misunderstands what we are trying to say, we stress.

We have been playing the survival game all of our lives, creating danger where danger doesn't exist, creating stress where stress isn't necessary. We must become aware of the way we function.

If we play the cause and effect game then ultimately the one cause for everything that happens and exists now was The Big Bang or God creating the universe (whichever you believe). Everything else after that was the effect of this one event.

Therefore, we can't take this scientific game of cause and effect and play it as a social game because then all we have is a world of effects, which leaves everyone powerless game pieces on a chess board.

In the social world, cause and effect doesn't determine fact. If I commit a crime, I go to prison. That is not a fact. I might get away with it, I might die before I go to prison or

I might flee the country. Therefore, it is not a fact that if I commit a crime, I will go to prison. It is a societal rule and might not even apply in other countries. It might even depend on the crime, my mental state and whom I killed. I might commit a crime in the jungles of Brazil and no one would ever know.

However, if I stand in front of a speeding train, I will get hit. It won't matter whether I was a good person or if I had good intentions. The train won't care who I am or what I am. The laws of physics won't change because of who you are. Cause and effect can easily be predicted in science because they rarely ever change.

We apply this same notion to our social world and to each other. We act, and instead of seeing that act as a cause, we see that as an effect. For instance, I go off and kill someone. The person's family sees my action as cause and the death as the effect. However, I might see it as the person deceiving me as the cause and my killing them as the effect of the deceit. Which one is the cause and which one is the effect?

We seem to be identifying our actions as effects instead of causes. Each effect is also a cause because the effect will cause another effect and so on.

We live our lives like dominos. Once we get pushed, we push the person in front of us. And when the person in front of us turns around and asks us why we pushed them, we blame the person behind us for having pushed us in the first place.

We can't blame other people for our reactions. You are not a domino; you are not a mechanical preprogrammed robot. You are a conscious being that chooses his or her actions.

Your negative beliefs about other people are not facts. When we confuse our beliefs as facts, because we used scientific cause and effect to determine those facts, we begin to justify our reactions toward them.

My mother once told me the story of two families who had spent decades killing each other because years before, one family member had killed a member of the other family.

The family took revenge and killed someone from the other family. The cycle of reaction, revenge and violence claimed the lives of countless people. Much like the Tumanyan story *A Drop of Honey*, people reacted to reactions and a chain of violence was created. Neither side took responsibility for their actions, and both sides blamed the other.

Ultimately, does it matter which side was right and which was wrong? There are no winners in a situation like that. Both sides believe that they are right in their actions. However, what does it matter if they are dead?

Someone once told me that a person who dies when they are right, might just as well have died when they were wrong because it doesn't matter either way when they are dead.

Much like a war that can never be won as soon as one life dies as a result of it, there are no winners in violence; only losers.

Say one person from one of those families remained in the end. Does that mean they won? What did they win? Did they win honor? What is honor exactly? Moreover, what is it worth in a situation like that? Is the worth all the lives of your family members?

We create many of our truths. If we believe that reputation and honor are more important than life, then we will act as if it is true and use violence and force against others who threaten it.

Then, after we sacrifice our loved ones, our peace of mind and our happiness, all we will have is reputation and honor. What will that do for us? Fill us up with pride?

The thing about pride is that it requires a constant feeding. It is easily attacked and can be easily injured. Then we are left with having to take drastic action to restore it. We use up our efforts and energies, and we sacrifice relationships trying to restore something that only exists in our minds.

When you are full of pride, people can easily make you do things you would not normally do by attacking your pride. "If you were really a man, you would…" "If you were a good friend, you would …"

You become susceptible to others' manipulation. If you are confident in who you are, then you don't require validity from others. Nor does it change who you are, just because someone else said otherwise.

It is entirely astonishing how much of our actions and reactions toward others are nothing but reactions to our own beliefs, decisions and facts that only exist in our minds.

QUOTE:

"The greatest deception men suffer is from their own opinions." - Leonardo da Vinci

“Happiness”

“The foolish man seeks happiness in the distance; the wise grows it under his feet.” -James Oppenheim

There was a point in my life when I was very driven. I was somewhat of an overachiever. I believed that if I was accomplished, then I would be happy. I never took the time to enjoy anything I accomplished, I just moved on to the next thing on my list. It left me feeling empty.

I was a published author, I owned my own clothing company, I was touring Los Angeles with my band, I was a youth leader for a women's group and I had a full-time job at Los Angeles Juvenile Probation Department. I did all of that at the age of 21.

My job paid me enough to buy anything I wanted. I even leased a little red convertible.

My schedule was packed full of many activities, both social and business. I attended concerts, parties (some of which my band played) and clubs. I even took seminars for self-improvement and leadership.

I kept myself very busy, but I wasn't happy. In fact, I kept myself so busy that I didn't even have the time to reflect on how unhappy I really was.

Nothing I did on the outside made me feel happy on the inside. Something felt as though it was missing.

What I was physically doing had nothing to do with what I wanted. I was seeking happiness by doing things and accumulating things.

Then I became ill. My band fell apart, I lost my friends, I lost my clothing company, I stopped attending my monthly group meetings for the women's group and I left my work. I lost my income and I lost my car.

It seemed like within a short period, everything fell apart. All of these things might seem negative, but they were all blessings in disguise.

My lifestyle was not making me happy. Since I was unwilling to change it consciously, my body did it through illness.

My subconscious wish was fulfilled and my life received an enormous overhaul. I lost all of the things I identified as my life and started a new one. My old life was over and a new one had begun.

When my illness was gone, I woke up to a completely different life. My life was different not because those "things" were gone but because my old way of thinking was. I was a different person, with different thoughts and values.

I no longer cared about impressing other people with my accomplishments. I also let go of trying to please others because their opinions of me were no longer more important than my opinion of myself.

QUOTE:

"fame or integrity: which is more important?
money or happiness: which is more valuable?
success or failure: which is more destructive?

if you look to others for fulfillment,
you will never truly be fulfilled,
if your happiness depends on money,
you will never be happy with yourself,

be content with what you have,
rejoice in the way things are,
when you realize there is nothing lacking,
the whole world belongs to you."
-Tao Te Ching

RECOGNIZING HAPPINESS:

"Happiness is the absence of striving for happiness." - Chang-Tzu

What does happiness look like? Does it look like someone surrounded by things, living in a big house or driving an expensive car?

Is it physical or materialistic? Is it the nice clothes they wear or the vacations they take? Is it the loudness of their laughter or the lavishness of their stories?

When you look at someone who is happy, what do you notice first?

Is there a sense of calm and a sense of togetherness about the person? Is there a bright energy that reflects in their eyes and their smile? Is there something indescribable about them that says they are happy, calm and peaceful?

Some wonder how we can be happy in a world that has war, hate and violence. We're not suffering because it's happening. It's happening because we're suffering.

Suffering, like happiness, is a state of mind. It's a perspective. It is a choice. Pain, on the other hand, isn't always a choice. We can't confuse the two. We suffer because we don't know how to deal with the pain.

Adrian White, from the United Kingdom's University of Leicester, did a study about the happiest places on earth. One of the top three happiest places on earth was Switzerland, the country that has been neutral in every war in the last two hundred years.

Happy people don't wage war, hate or become violent. It's not in their nature because their state of being has shifted toward happiness.

They're not happy people because they don't fight wars, they don't fight wars because they are happy people.

They don't carry cravings and they don't confuse pleasures with happiness.

Let's break down a few things …

Suffering: anxiety, fatigue, depression, anger, constant craving.

Cravings: drugs, alcohol, gambling, smoking, compulsive shopping, compulsive sex.

Pleasures: family, friends, career, money, things.

Happiness: internal state of mind that does not rely on outside factors. Regardless of what occurs, the state of being does not change.

Cars fall under pleasures because they are pleasurable to some people and a pain to other people.

You may believe that a new car is going to make you happy but instead the car has multiple problems and ends up costing you hundreds of dollars in repairs. You might even end up in a car accident and hurt. Will that make you happy?

But since different things cause different reactions in different people, then no one thing can guarantee happiness. Children, marriage, cars, houses or money, none of these things are guaranteed to make anyone happy.

We confuse these pleasures for happiness. It's a pleasure to be with your family and friends, hopefully, but it's not happiness unless you already are happy.

Outside factors don't determine happiness. Happiness determines outside factors.

Things don't "cause" happiness. We cause the feeling in ourselves because we bought those things. We take pleasure in those things and we confuse pleasure with real happiness.

Since happiness is based in the mind and not external circumstances, you can be happy for no reason and anytime you choose regardless of any outside circumstance.

We get preoccupied wanting the physical thing that we believe will give us happiness, not realizing that if our default state of mind is happiness, then nothing can interfere with it.

If my default state is one of anger, then I will feel angry, frustrated and upset most of the time. Then I will get happy, experience pleasure for a short period and then revert to my default state of mind.

However, if my default state of mind is happiness, then regardless of what occurs, I will always revert to my happiness.

When we see someone who is happy, we see that they are not only happy with their life but also with who they are.

Happiness requires you to be yourself. This means that you must stop wanting someone else's life, body, car, talent or features.

You must want you. You must choose your life and everything in it. If you hate, fight or struggle against what is, you will not be happiness.

Why do we want to be someone or something else? Is it because we believe people won't like us as we are and therefore we should be like other people? If your happiness depends on the views of other people, you will suffer. If you have no confidence in yourself, when others don't recognize you as beautiful or worthy, you will suffer.

Humans are the only creatures who fight against their own nature and try to be something else.

What if all cows wanted to be horses and they stopped producing milk? What if all roses wanted to be carnations? What would happen to their beauty?

Nothing in nature fights its own nature the way humans do.

There is but one you. Why destroy something so unique because you believe someone else's uniqueness is better than yours?

You can't be happy as someone else because you can never be anyone else except yourself. The choice is either to be happy as you or suffer trying to be happy as someone else.

If you were to look in the mirror right now, would you recognize happiness within yourself?

"Happiness"

QUOTE:
"People spend a lifetime searching for happiness; looking for peace. They chase idle dreams, addictions, religions, even other people, hoping to fill the emptiness that plagues them. The irony is the only place they ever needed to search was within." -Ramona L. Anderson

---

POSSESSIONS:
"He is rich or poor according to what he is, not according to what he has." -Henry Ward Beecher

I watched a documentary on children in Central Africa who do not have access to clean water. They were poor and didn't own any toys or things. They worked together to get work done around the village and they used things in nature to create games. They were happy even though they didn't own anything.

I then thought of all the children I have observed around me. They have plenty of things, the latest electronic gadgets, clothes and toys. They don't have to worry about clean water, food on the table or even having a table.

In our society, children throw fits over toys, TV, clothes and food choices. They cry when their toys break or when they don't get what they want.

The children I watched in the documentary didn't have anything to cry about. They didn't have a choice of clothes so they were happy to wear the same thing every day. They ate whatever was available that day and they were grateful for the little they did have to eat.

They didn't have objects to fight over and they shared a strong sense of community. They all looked after each other and I don't recall seeing any of those children sad, mad or upset over their situations.

They had big smiles on their faces, they couldn't stop laughing and enjoying the life they had while they had it. They didn't have much, based on our standards, but they were happy.

It seems like the more we have, the unhappier we are. We can see it in our children. They have insatiable appetites for things.

We work hard to give our children everything they want and yet that leaves them unsatisfied and unhappy.

We seek out certain things. We yearn for them, want them, lust after them and sometimes greedily pursue them: Money, cars, love, success, security. We focus on cravings and pleasures, thinking that they will lead to happiness.

In reality, we don't want any of these things. We want happiness. We have somehow convinced ourselves that if we had the right car, the right house or the right income, that we would be happy.

When in reality, you don't need any of those things to be happy.

I believe that we were not placed on this planet to buy cars and earn money. That is something we learned from others who were here before we were born. At some point in our lives, we decided that those things were the road to happiness. We see others riding in their nice cars and living in their big homes and we believe that they are happy *because* they have these things. Who is to say why they are happy and if they are in fact happy?

Who can really know whether someone else is truly happy?

"Happiness"

On the outside, my life seemed very exciting and rich. I was rich with friends, activity, laughter and income. Was I successful? Yes. Was I happy? No.

Success is getting what you want. Happiness is wanting what you have. I had things, but I didn't really want them. They didn't mean much to me but I couldn't turn off my need for more.

I realize now that it's not how much you have, but how much you enjoy. I did not enjoy my life or the things in my life because I was concerned with having more.

You have things in your life now. Are you happy? Can you remember a time before you had those things? Do you remember when you believed that you would be happy if you bought them?

How long did it take before you wanted a different car or purse? How long did it take before you were over your new phone or your new clothes?

We have a tendency to want things because we believe that once we have them, we will have happiness as well.

Even when you have everything, you will find something else to want. Even billionaires don't stop wanting things after they make billions. They still strive for more, want more and get more. Making a lot of money wasn't the ultimate goal because if it were, there would be nothing else to want after that. So then, money isn't the goal. Happiness is. After all, most of us believe that money buys happiness. So why would you want that much money if you didn't want an endless supply of happiness?

Most of the actions we perform on a daily basis are because we believe they will make us happy. We work hard to make money because we believe we will be happy if we had money and bought things. We get married and have children because we believe it will bring us happiness.

I had reasons behind what I was doing. I didn't do it because I loved doing it. I did it for acceptance, attention or love.

I also believed that if I had acceptance, attention or love that I would be happy. However, once I received the attention from my achievements, once I received the acceptance and the love, I was still unhappy.

There was always that underlining reason that had nothing to do with the actual act that I was performing. For instance, when I picked up the guitar, I did it for the attention or praise I believed would bring me happiness, not because I loved music and loved playing the guitar.

I did not do things out of love; I did things because I believed they would bring me happiness.

There was always a hidden motive behind the things I was doing. I was working, not because I loved my job, but because I needed the money. I played on stage, not because I wanted to share my music and voice with the world, but because I craved attention. I achieved not because I loved the things I did, but because I needed acceptance and praise.

I wanted all of those underlining things because I believed that those things would bring me happiness.

If I had enough attention, acceptance, or love, maybe then I would be happy. Unfortunately, regardless of how much I received, it never felt like it was enough.

Now, however, I play the guitar because I love making music. I write because I enjoy it. There is no underlining motive. I do things out of love, not out of out premeditative hidden reasons.

"Happiness"

We all have a false belief regarding happiness. Most of us believe that we can be happy when …

I will be happy when I'm rich. I will be happy when I buy this car. I will be happy when I get married.

We believe these internal statements even though they fail us continuously. How many times have you told yourself that you will be happy when something happens?

It seems as though we wait for some other outside factor to make us happy instead of looking within.

If you're always angry, the circumstances will not change to make you happy. Therefore, if you are always happy, the circumstances will not change to make you unhappy. It is you, not the circumstances.

The circumstances have changed several times before and you can still find reasons to be angry. You must not fight to change your circumstances; angry doesn't go away through fighting, it goes away through acceptance.

Angry people don't accept anything, and that is why they are angry. They are angry because they believe things should be different than they are. Unfortunately, regardless of what changes or how it changes, they still feel as if it should be different.

There are people in their situation who are happy. Several different people work the same job or work at the same office, some are happy and some are angry. Siblings can grow up in the same house depressed or happy.

If you always do what you've always done, you'll always get what you've always gotten. If your happiness depends on your circumstances or other people then something else will always be in the driver's seat of your life.

It is not the situation but how you see the situation. Happiness is not a destination. You will not go there and then always be happy. Happiness isn't something you can hold onto or try not to lose like a necklace.

Happiness is perception. It's a pair of glasses you put on that filters everything you see through happiness.

If you can do it with anger, sadness, paranoia, and skepticism, then you can do it with happiness. So the question is why don't you?

Is it just easier being angry? Perhaps it's the fear of losing happiness that stops you from being or enjoying happiness.

Since happiness is a perception and not a physical thing or person, then you can't lose it if you don't want to lose it. It's your decision.

Anyone in any circumstance can be happy if they choose to do so.

QUOTE:
"We tend to forget that happiness doesn't come as a result of getting something we don't have, but rather of recognizing and appreciating what we do have." - Frederick Koenig

---

ADAPTATION:
"Adapt or perish, now as ever, is nature's inexorable imperative." -H. G. Wells

Adaptation is what helps humans survive in this world. It means that we can find the harshest environments, from the hot Sahara desert to the freezing Siberian landscapes, and we can make it our home.

Adaptation is also the reason why we cannot achieve happiness through things or people.

"Happiness"

Regardless of how many things we have or how much money we have, we can adapt to it, making it feel normal.

The first initial response to receiving something might be one of excitement, joy and pleasure. However, those feelings cannot be sustained over time with the same things. New things are required to re-stimulate those emotions. Much like drugs, once the initial stimulation has worn away, another dose is needed.

We cannot rely on things to make us happy. Whether we lived in a hut in a remote region with no technology or in Beverly Hills with every form of technological advances, we can be happy.

There are thousands of people living without technology or things and they are happy. So then, why do we assume we need things to make us happy?

Regardless of the situation, you can adapt. There was a time when the telephone was first invented and people believed it would change the whole world. There was excitement and hope. Now, we take the telephone for granted. It's around us all the time and we don't think twice about it. The same goes for cars, the Internet, the stove, refrigerators, etc.

We've adapted to living with these things and we're not "happy" even though we have them. In fact, they have been so integrated into our lives that we don't even think about them, even when we use them.

A new car, a new house or the new gadget will become normal after a short period and we will go back to feeling the way we normally feel. After that, our minds will set itself upon another gadget it believes will make us happy.

This is why we must make happiness our normal state of mind. It won't require money, possessions or actions to keep it.

Happiness doesn't require you to feed it. Greed does.

Greed is bottomless. It can never be filled or satisfied. Having more only requires more. It is an insatiable feeling that makes you believe you will not be happy unless you acquire the thing you want. The irony is that it can never be filled.

Greed gives a momentary satisfaction to sustain you, but then it becomes empty again.

Regardless of how much we have, we can adapt to it and make it normal. In the same way, a person can adapt to not having much money or things. Both can be happy and both can suffer.

When we try to find happiness through things, we suffer when we lose them. We even suffer when we think about losing them. It leaves us in a state of paranoia, anxiety and fear.

We fear losing things because we believe that they hold our happiness.

Happiness must come from the self. It cannot exist externally. If a person is not happy, no amount of things will change that.

All things become habitual. So when that "magic" thing happens that is supposed to make you happy forever, you get used to it and back you go to searching for the next thing you believe will make you happy.

In order to be happy, we must shift our perspective about life and about ourselves. It is how we view ourselves, others and the world that determines whether we are happy.

A happy person does not look at life as a competition for shiny things. A happy person does not view the world as a chaotic mess full of races and people who want him to fail or die. How can anyone be happy with viewpoints that cause anxiety, fear, anger, defensiveness and aggression?

Both happiness and suffering come from within the individual and are not dependent on outside factors. We must shift ourselves and not resist life. To resist change is to resist the process of life. This is the source of suffering.

You can be happy and still experience other emotions. Happiness is not the absence of sadness. Happiness is not non-stop bliss. Happiness is the acceptance of life, change and all of the surprises they bring.

When you feel anger or sadness, allow yourself to feel it, accept it and then release it. It's when we make ourselves wrong for feeling the emotions that allows them to linger.

We get mad and then we stay mad because we hate the fact that we became mad. When you feel mad, it doesn't make you an awful person, it just makes you human. Acknowledge the emotion and move through it.

Feel it and then release it. When we fight to repress our emotions, it feeds suffering. It causes stress and frustration.

Suffering derives from non-acceptance. That means that you must also accept the emotions you feel. If you make yourself wrong for every negative emotion you feel, you will never be able to release negative emotions. Getting mad will make you feel bad about yourself. Feeling bad about yourself will make you feel sad. Feeling sad will make you frustrated that you can't be happy. It is a cycle of negativity that can easily be stopped by accepting whatever emotion you feel whenever you feel it.

Happiness and suffering are internal. It's just a matter of which one you choose as your state of mind.

If your happiness is given to you by outside circumstances, then it can be taken away from you by outside circumstances. If happiness is your state of mind, no circumstance can take it away from you.

Once happiness is the "normal" state of mind, then regardless of what events take place, the mind will always return to its normal state. Then and only then can we be truly happy.

QUOTE:
"But what is happiness except the simple harmony between a man and the life he leads?" -Albert Camus

---

THE WORLD OF WEALTH:
"Only after the last tree has been cut down. Only after the last river has been poisoned. Only after the last fish has been caught. Only then you will find that money cannot be eaten." -Cree Indian Prophesy

We have been classically conditioned to believe that certain things are good while others are bad. We have automatic responses to information we receive.

For example, winning the lottery is an automatic positive response even though the winner is unaware of the problems and troubles that may come with it.

A man named William Post won $16.2 million in the Pennsylvania lottery in 1988. However, he now lives on his Social Security.

Post even told newspapers that it was a nightmare. He had a series of lawsuits, including a past girlfriend who successfully sued him for a share of his winnings.

His brother was arrested for hiring a hit man to kill him, hoping to inherit a share of the winnings. His other siblings harassed him until he agreed to invest in a car business and a restaurant in Sarasota, Fla., - two ventures that brought back no money and further strained his relationship with his siblings.

Within a year, he was $1 million in debt. He even spent time in jail for firing a gun over the head of a bill collector.

He eventually declared bankruptcy and lives on food stamps.

He later told a newspaper, "I'm tired, I'm over 65 years old and I just had a serious operation for a heart aneurysm. Lotteries don't mean (anything) to me."

So was William Post's experience good or bad? Some might say that it was good that he won the lottery but bad because of what happened.

Mr. Post learned a very valuable lesson that we often don't get the chance to learn. He needed to win the lottery to know that he didn't need to win the lottery.

Many times, we strongly believe that we "need" something. We will be happy only if circumstances were different. Mr. Post learned that money did not guarantee happiness.

Could he have possibly foreseen any of these events? No. He did not know what that which he was asking for would bring. He assumed that money would bring happiness.

Many times, we seek outside things because we feel empty inside. We numb ourselves to the emptiness through alcohol, drugs, things, food, sex, etc.

In the United States, we have a growing epidemic of obesity. It seems as if we can't quite get full. My question is, is this a physical, emotional, mental or a spiritual problem? I believe it is all of the above.

All over the world, 963 million people are hungry.[1] Every day, almost 16,000 children die from hunger-related causes - one child every five seconds.[2]

We in the U.S. overeat, become obese and then spend thousands of dollars on a surgical procedure to get a band placed around our stomachs so that we can eat less.

The diet industry is a multi-billion dollar industry in the United States. We are worrying about losing weight while the rest of the world is starving.

However, we are not immune to the issue of hunger either. 35.5 million people -- including 12.6 million children -- live in households that experience hunger or the risk of hunger. This represents more than one in ten households in the United States (10.9 percent).[3]

We have food available to us everywhere we go, so we don't appreciate what we have. In fact, we throw away most of it.

If we lived in a hunting society where we only ate if we successfully hunted our food, we would appreciate every ounce of what we ate. We would eat less and we would be grateful for what we had because it took time and energy.

We are the fastest growing nation for obesity. However, we can't seem to fill ourselves up, regardless of how much we eat. We are also a sex-obsessed, drug-dependent, consuming society. Our greed for instant pleasure has left us unhappy.

We must distinguish between cravings, pleasure and happiness so that we do not continue believing that outside factors can bring us happiness.

We must be aware that we use pleasure to fill emptiness and hide unhappiness. It is the only way we can begin to shift our focus, attention and actions.

"Happiness"

Have you ever thought, I'll be happy when I'm rich?

If you make $5,000 a year, you are within the top 15 percent of the world's richest people. That means that 85 percent of the world's population is beneath your economic level.

If you make $10,000 a year, you are within the top 13 percent of the world's richest people. That means that 87 percent of the world's population is beneath your economic level.

If you make $25,000 a year, you are within the top 10 percent of the world's richest people. That means that 90 percent of the world's population is beneath your economic level.

If you make $50,000 a year, you are within the top 0.98 percent of the world's richest people. That's less than one percent. That means that 99 percent of the world's population is beneath your economic level and only 59 million people are above your economic level.

Moreover, if you are at the top of America's middle class and make $200,000 a year, you are within the top 0.01 percent of the world's richest people.

Congratulations, you are rich. You just didn't realize it before. Are you happy now? Will you remain happy tomorrow when you have to wake up and go to work?

I hope that you will feel appreciation for the income you currently have and begin the process of being happy with your current state without identifying with it or feeling so attached to it that you will emotionally crumble if you no longer made that amount.

You are now, by comparison, rich. Perhaps, believing that wealth will bring happiness is not about being rich. Perhaps it's about having more.

Greed, by definition, means never being satisfied with what you have. It is the opposite of what it means to be happy.

Poor people and rich people want more; greed doesn't discriminate between economic classes. Greed doesn't allow us to be happy. After all, you are now rich.

You may not be as rich as you believe you should be, but in comparison to the rest of the world's population, you are rich. What more do you want?

I can bet that there are more things you want. A better this, a better that. A bigger this and a bigger that. We always feel that we need more money.

Three billion people live on less than $2 per day while 1.3 billion live on less than $1 per day. Additionally, 70 percent of those living on less than $1 per day are women.

At the time of this writing, a non-working American on disability receives approximately $900 per month. That's $10,800 a year. That means that an American on disability is richer than 87 percent of the world's population.

The poor in America are richer than the rich in other countries. It's a matter of perspective.

If you currently make $2,000 a month and your monthly expenses are about that much, you won't feel very rich. However, if you made $10,000 a month and your monthly expenses were $11,000, you certainly will not feel rich either. In fact, you won't be able to enjoy much of what you have because you will feel stress and anxiety over your financial situation.

So, is it a matter of how much you make or how much you spend? Because the rich can tell you that being rich isn't that big of a deal when your expenses are high.

Using the statistics from earlier, the majority of the people I know are rich. They complain about money frequently and each one of them wants to make more money than they currently earn. Their incomes range from $1,200 per month to $40,000 per month.

At some point, we stop wanting more of what we have, and we want more than what other people have.

We are subconsciously invested in competing against each other and playing a game of one-upmanship. I'm smarter, I'm better looking, I have more money.

It's not enough to be smart, good looking or have money, we always want more than other people. Then when we come across people who have more than we do, we become upset, jealous or we feel the need to put them down to make ourselves feel better.

This doesn't end with just things, money or characteristics. This game is also played with God. I'm more spiritual than you. My religion is better than yours. I know more about God than you do. Etc.

It's not enough to believe in God or practice our religion, we feel compelled to compete against others and prove that our beliefs are right. We want to feel superior.

What do we gain from this? Even if we do feel superior now, we will meet someone who has more than we do and then back we go to feeling low, jealous or angry.

For the sake of argument, let's say you do have more than others do. So what does that mean? Does that mean you are better than them now?

Since when has having more meant that someone is superior? In addition, if it does mean that you are now superior, then what? What happens after you're better than others?

We collect things to make our lives or ourselves better but we are not better for it. What's wrong with what you have now? Why does everything require an upgrade?

I can find another human being who would be more than happy to trade places with you. I can find someone who would be happy to have the income you're unsatisfied with, the spouse you wish were different, the body you hate or the life that makes you unhappy.

How long do we play this game of having more than others? What does it accomplish other than to feed our ego, make us feel superior and keep us unhappy?

If happiness is the acceptance of what is, then playing the game of having more than others can only keep us unhappy all the time. There will always be someone else who has more.

Having more has nothing to do with wealth. Wealth, I believe, is a matter of happiness. A happy person is a wealthy person. This is the opposite of what we currently believe. We believe that a wealthy person is a happy person.

A person who is happy is rich with love and peace and radiates those things on everyone around them. A wealthy person is not dependent on things and money to fill them up.

Greed leaves you feeling as if you never have enough. Greed makes you competitive and leaves you unsatisfied. You may not feel as though you are greedy, but do your actions say otherwise?

Look around at what you have. Stop for a moment and really look around at what you have. Can you remember a time when you didn't have any of those things and you believed that if you had them, you would be happy? So why is it that you want more?

What is it that makes you believe that more things will equal more happiness?

QUOTE:
"Too many people spend money they haven't earned, to buy things they don't want, to impress people they don't like." -Will Rogers

----

Hunger Statistics from bread.org

[1] State of Food Insecurity in the World, 2008 FAO."Food Security Statistics". www.fao.org/es/ess/faostat/foodsecurity/index_en.htm

[2] Black, Robert, Morris, Saul, & Jennifer Bryce. "Where and Why Are 10 Million Children Dying Every Year?" *The Lancet* 361:2226-2234. 2003.

[3] *Household Food Security in the United States, 2005.* USDA Economic Research Service. November 2006

Financial Statistical Sources:

1. World Bank Development Research Group
2. Globalrichlist.com
3. 2003 world population Data Sheet of the Population Reference Bureau.
4. Steven Mosher, president of the population research institute, CNN, October 13, 1999.
5. Milanovic, Branco. "True World Income Distribution", 1988 and 1993: World Bank Development Research Group, November 2000, page 30.

RELATIONSHIPS:
"Consider the following. We humans are social beings. We come into the world as the result of others' actions. We survive here in dependence on others. Whether we like it or not, there is hardly a moment of our lives when we do not benefit from others' activities. For this reason, it is hardly surprising that most of our happiness arises in the context of our relationships with others." -The Dalai Lama

Relationships are an important aspect of happiness. When we accept others as they are, we stop fighting and struggling to change them. Most of the unhappiness we feel toward others is a result of our rejection of who they are.

Most people, when they hear the word relationship, assume that relationships are only in the romantic variety.

We have relationships with family members, friends, co-workers, neighbors, taxi drivers, store clerks, receptionists, etc.

If happiness is acceptance, then we must not forget that it also applies to the people in our lives as well.

Once we accept ourselves, our income and everything else in our lives, we must then accept the people in our lives. This is crucial. We cannot be happy if we are stuck trying to change other people.

Be grateful for the people who make you angry or upset, they show you the weakness in your character.

We cannot be happy unless we stop trying to change people. Why should others change just because we believe they should be different?

I, personally, would not want others to fight and struggle to change me into their idea of a better me. Would you? Yet we do it to others all the time.

Our culture has taught us from a young age that we should change for others and therefore we can make others change for us.

We all believe that other people would be better off if they became our version of themselves.

Since we cannot see beneath the surface of each individual and don't know the inner complicated workings of each world, how can we possibly know what would be better for others? We may mettle, create the opposite of our desired goal and cause unhappiness all around.

Giving advice is easy. We already arrogantly believe that we know better than others do and that others would greatly benefit from our knowledge. However, understanding and compassion are the difficult parts and yet they are the most needed.

The highest level of happiness is achieved through compassion for others.

We all feel like we know better than others do even when it comes to their own lives. If only people listened to our advice, they would be better off.

I hear people say it all the time, if they only had someone else's money or looks or life then they would live it better.

Can you think of someone's life that you could live better? A friend, neighbor, family member, someone who you think isn't doing such a good job living their own life?

Just because something or someone doesn't do what you planned or expected, doesn't mean it's wrong or it failed.

You can't be sure how your advice or interference will affect the other person's life. We can never fully understand the inner workings of another individual. We don't live inside their mind, heart or world.

A Second Opinion

Sometimes the people with the best intentions can cause the biggest damage by trying to control or steer someone else's feelings, goals or life.

I am not offering you advice. I don't know you and cannot predict how my advice might affect your life.

This book is not intended to change who you are. It is another option available for the road to peace, happiness and the end of suffering.

Once you unload all of the negative Self-Talk, destructive emotions, false beliefs and all of the other excessive things you've picked up along the way, you can be free to be yourself. But only if you choose to be.

Ultimately, it would be unwise for me to advise you to do anything. We can never really predict how things will turn out. Therefore, it is on you to find your way and which tools you decide to use.

I can offer different perspectives, opinions and options, but in the end, the decision is yours. Your life and wellbeing is your responsibility. The only thing I can offer is a second opinion.

You are responsible for yourself and your happiness. No one else is responsible for your happiness. In fact, I couldn't make you happy even if I wanted to.

We must distinguish between bringing happiness to others and trying to make others happy. This is an important distinction.

Some people make themselves unhappy by struggling to make others happy. Parents overbuy things for their children believing that it will make them happy. The children don't appreciate what they receive because they are bombarded with things. Parents then feel unappreciated, overworked and stressed. Both parties are left unhappy.

"Happiness"

We don't feel happy and yet we use the same methods that don't make us happy to try to make others happy.

As simple as it may sound, the best way to bring happiness to others is to be happy yourself. It is the only way to bring it. After all, if you aren't it, how can you bring it? You bring it when you bring yourself.

People continue to feel happy when they bring happiness to others. Happy people feel compelled to share happiness and when others become happy, this reinforces their happiness. This is a positive cycle.

Studies have found that disaster relief victims who help other victims of the disaster bounce back to normal faster than those who don't.

It appears that being happy is contagious. Just by being our happy selves, we can set an example for those around to follow suit. And once the people around us are their happy selves, we can continue to feel our unbound joy.

So, it appears that our happiness is automatically spread to those around us without our intentional doing. Moreover, witnessing their happiness seems to amplify our happiness.

Wouldn't it make you feel happier knowing that you bring happiness to everyone around just by being yourself? No strings attached, no money involved, no intentions; just you being you.

Best of all, happiness is in abundance. It never runs out. A candle that lights other candles will not lose its flame by sharing it. So bringing happiness to others only strengthens yours.

QUOTE:
"Those who bring sunshine into the lives of others cannot keep it from themselves."- James M. Barrie

“Meaning”

“All meaning is self-created.” -Virginia Satir

Our minds are creating machines. It creates meaning in everything.

Objects, symbols and images hold certain meanings for us. When we see this symbol, $, we know that it holds a specific meaning. Religious symbols, road signs and other images hold meanings as well. When we see a white dove, we know it means peace.

However, our minds don't stop creating meanings outside of symbols. Whether it is an argument, the tone of someone's voice, the way someone looked at you, an action, a behavior or a simple comment. We make meanings out of everything around us.

Usually, the meanings we create are personal. This is what makes someone else's comments, behaviors or actions feel personal for us.

It can cause problems within relationships because simple things can "mean" much more complicated things.

For instance, if you and I were in an argument and you raised your voice at me, I might make that mean that you think I'm stupid.

After that, I might hold it against you and feel anger toward you, but not because you yelled at me, but because you think I'm stupid. I will remember the meaning, not the act.

A large majority of suffering derives not from events, but from the meanings we give events.

We place meaning on things, events and situations, and we become upset as a result of our meanings.

For instance, when someone leaves us, we may not be upset because they left; we might be upset because it means that they didn't really love us enough to stay. Does it really mean that or do we make it mean that?

Some people think that when a man is jealous, it means that he really loves his wife or girlfriend. Who decided that meaning? Psychologists believe that jealousy is a symptom of low self-esteem and no confidence.

I heard a woman talk about how her life was over because she had been diagnosed with cancer. Getting cancer didn't mean her life was over. She made it mean that. Just like winning the lottery doesn't mean you will no longer have any problems.

I used to believe that getting attention meant that I was getting love. The more attention I received the more I believed I was loved. It never occurred to me that my need for attention was making me create that meaning.

These meanings are so deep and so much a part of our subconscious, it requires awareness to see them.

It is far easier to catch yourself creating meaning during the event or just after an event.

"Meaning"

Many times during the event, when we feel upset, we make verbal statements that can show us what we subconsciously believe the event means.

When we look back at the event, we think of the meaning we created for the event. When we remember and cry, we are not crying for the event, we are crying for the meaning.

Events are not painful; our meanings for events are painful. We can't always choose events, but we can always choose the meaning.

Some people choose to make negative events mean that they are supposed to learn a valuable lesson from the event and they suffer less because of the meaning.

Some people make negative events mean that they did something awful and are being punished for it therefore, they deserve to suffer.

If five people are a part of the same event, does that mean they have the same experience or that the event means the same thing for all?

Each person brings with them a different world; a world containing unique memories, feelings, thoughts, dreams, hopes and goals.

If five people go on a journey together, they each begin at a different point and end at a different end. Even if they are together physically throughout the entire trip, internally, they are worlds apart.

Each will leave the experience having gained a different memory, lesson, meaning and experience.

Your experience is real and unique to you. If the Blind Men who touched different parts of the elephant took turns and touched the same part, they would still have different experiences. It would "mean" something different for each.

How much of our lives are self-created meanings? Even if there was a higher meaning and purpose for our lives that we are unaware of, what good would that do us if we were running around creating negative meanings for our lives and acting as if they were true?

What would this higher purpose serve if we constantly sabotaged it by creating negative meanings, thinking self-defeating thoughts, feeling terrible about ourselves, hating our lives and acting as if it's all true?

Once we accept that meaning is self-created, we can significantly alter how we view our lives and what it all means. After all, the only important meaning of life is the one we choose to give it.

QUOTE:
"If the whole universe has no meaning, we should never have found out that it has no meaning: just as, if there were no light in the universe and therefore no creatures with eyes, we should never know it was dark. Dark would be without meaning." - C.S. Lewis

---

OPPORTUNITIES FOR GROWTH:
"When you're finished changing, you're finished."
-Benjamin Franklin

The greatest understandings and epiphanies come from illness, tragedy and loss. They are opportunities for growth and enlightenment.

I, personally, have found that illness is a great opportunity for growth. It is the one thing that can rip you out of the routine of your daily life and force you to reexamine your life, beliefs, feelings, relationships and thoughts.

We all experience these things. We cannot fight life. Life is a process that cannot be fought.

Something must die in order for something new to be born. Life must first get rid of one thing to open space for another.

We get frustrated when we fight the process. We use the partial knowledge that we have accumulated to fight and control the process. If we fight life, we suffer.

Imagine if the caterpillar fought life’s process and did not go into the cocoon. What would happen if the caterpillar decided that it was just too scary to live inside a dark lonely cocoon for months?

However, the caterpillar knows that the dark and the lonely is a part of the process of becoming a butterfly, therefore he does it willingly and without a fight.

The caterpillar will become a butterfly only after he gives up being a caterpillar.

We too need to give up certain ways of being in order to transform. When we are offered opportunities for growth, instead of fighting them, we must embrace them.

Every time you go through a “dark” period just know that you’re in the process of transformation. Don’t resist it.

That is the difference between the animals and humans. The animals go with the flow of life’s process and changes; we fight life’s process to the very end. We struggle with life because life offers us things we didn’t plan. Life takes us places we didn’t think about or want.

Some see things as bad or negative. They are only negative if you see them as negative.

Can we have definite good and bad? An accident for you might mean “bad” because of the damages caused by the accident. An accident for someone else might be considered one of the best things to ever happen to that person.

Imagine if a man gets into a car accident and hits his head. He is rushed to the hospital and given a head scan. The doctors discover a tumor, remove it and save the man's life. The tumor might not have been found in time if it had not been for the accident. The man can look back joyfully at the accident that saved his life. You may look back at the same accident as the other driver and curse your luck. Is the accident good or bad? It depends on whom you ask.

It's how we choose to look at things that determine their worth, their value, their importance and whether they are good or bad.

Good and bad exist in our experience. Even if we look at death, we can find different experiences. One may look at the death of a loved one as a tragedy while another may look at it as someone finally escaping a life of physical pain and anguish.

If an eighty-year-old man dies in his sleep after experiencing years of physical pain, we say that it was better that he died. When another person dies who was not in pain, perhaps younger than that man was, we say it was a tragedy.

Nevertheless, is it not the same act of death? Do we view them differently because we believe one is good and the other is bad? You might be able to say, "Well it depends." And you're right. If it depends on the situation and the people involved, then it makes the notions of good and bad easily arguable.

One might argue that killing another human being is wrong and bad and there is no argument for it. However, is that really how we have been taught to view killing?

If I walk up to someone and kill him or her because I don't like the race they were born into, is that wrong and bad? Do I have that right to kill them because their existence goes against my beliefs?

If I kill someone who is trying to kill me, is that wrong and bad?

What if I had a soldier's uniform on and killed during a war? Is that wrong and bad? Some give a hero's welcome to soldiers returning from war and praise them for keeping us safe while others might view the same people who committed the same acts as murderers or terrorists. Albert Einstein said "It is my conviction that killing under the cloak of war is nothing but an act of murder." One person's terrorist is another person's Freedom Fighter.

Three different situations and yet we have the same act. Why is it different? We make them different. We decide whether something is good or bad, right or wrong.

There are people in the world who believe the exact opposite of what you believe. Are they wrong for believing it? Perhaps you're wrong for believing it? It depends on whom we ask.

You may believe that your beliefs are right and that you know that they're right. But how do you know? Your experiences are validated by your filter. But the same can be said from the other person. To him, his experiences have been validating his beliefs.

The only difference is that you were born in one part of the Earth and they were born in another. Perhaps if you were born where they were born and believed the same things, the two of you may have been good friends.

You may point to all of the other people who believe the same as you do and say, "They believe it too. I must be right." But how do those other people know? Just because a group of people believes the same thing, doesn't make it any more true.

Have you ever wondered how is it that other people can believe what they believe when it's so obviously a lie, fake or not real? They wonder the same thing about you. Your beliefs to them are not real. They experience their beliefs and you experience yours. Who decides which one is real, good or true?

Why can't we all just believe different things? Why do we feel the need to make others believe what we believe?

There are things that seem bad and other things that seem good. It's different for different people. We are the ones to decide whether something is good or bad for us.

We'll See

An old farmer worked his crops every day. One day, his horse ran away. Upon hearing the news, his neighbors came to visit. "Such bad luck," they said sympathetically. "We'll see" the farmer smiled.

A few days later, the horse returned, bringing with it three other wild horses. His neighbors returned to congratulate him, "How wonderful!" the neighbors exclaimed. But the old farmer just smiled and replied "We'll see."

The following day, his son tried to ride one of the untamed horses, was thrown and broke his leg. The neighbors again came to offer their sympathy on his misfortune. The old farmer, once again, smiled and replied, "We'll see."

A week later, military officials came to the village to draft young men into the army. Seeing that the son's leg was broken, they let him stay behind. The neighbors congratulated the farmer on how well things had turned out.

"We'll see," said the farmer.

QUOTE:
"The meaning of things lies not in the things themselves, but in our attitude towards them." -Antoine de Saint-Exupery

---

SEPARATION:
"Enlightenment for a wave in the ocean is the moment the wave realizes that it is the ocean." -Thich Nhat Hanh

Is a wave separate from the ocean? When we see a wave, we can point and call it a wave and others will recognize what we are speaking about. However, is the wave not the ocean?

The wave is merely a distinction in our mind. We have separated the wave from the ocean because it's a different behavior for the ocean.

If the ocean created a larger wave, we would call it a tsunami. If the ocean tossed and turned, we would call it a tempest.

We already know that it is because of our innate ability to separate, label and judge that aids in our feelings of separation from the world around us. We have made enemies of the animals, the Earth and ourselves.

We are constantly battling other people, animals and the forces of nature. Are we really battling "other" things?

Without separation, there is no "other," there is no "them." There is only "us."

If we make ice sculptures of people, animals, places and things, aren't they all still just ice?

Whether it is rain, river, stream, ocean, lake, tsunami, wave, or ice, they are all water. They may have different names that we have created to label different actions and behaviors of water, but it is all still water.

White light can create the different colors of the rainbow. If you shine a white light into a prism, it will disperse many colors. When the sun shines onto droplets of moisture in the Earth's atmosphere it causes a colored variety of light to appear across the sky, also known as a rainbow.

Blue, red, yellow, green, they all contain the white light that created them.

If we see things as separate, then we start to deal with things as separate. We begin the fight to isolate one from another. We separate ourselves from everything and behave as if that is reality. We forget that we chose to separate ourselves.

We have separated ourselves from nature because we feel above nature. Our separation is in our mind. We are no more separated from nature than our hearts are separated from our kidneys. Everything is intertwined and connected.

We try to stand apart from nature in order to categorize and understand nature but we cannot actually stand apart from nature. Your mouth can't eat itself and you can't separate yourself from nature. Your mouth would have to step outside of itself to eat itself and you would have to step outside of yourself to step outside of nature.

We also try to separate pairs that cannot exist without each other. Like pleasure and pain. We see them as separate things and so we struggle to separate them.

To have pleasure without pain would be no pleasure at all. It would cause a mental state that would eliminate pleasure all together.

If we had all pleasure all the time, we would no longer be able to recognize pleasure. It would become normal and boring thus eliminating the very thing we seek.

We can't separate up from down, inside from outside, pleasure from pain. If we did, neither would exist. They exist because of their opposite.

We have bad in the world because we have good. We can't fight for peace, goodness, righteousness or freedom. All things we view as "threats" to them are being done by people who see themselves as good, peaceful, righteous people. No one sees themselves as evil or on the wrong side.

Even if you can point to a group and say that you are fighting them because they are evil, just know that when they fight you, they are thinking the same thing.

Terrorists don't view themselves as terrorists, they view themselves as Freedom Fighters. They are fighting a big evil empire called the United States. The U.S. sees them as evil; they see the U.S. as evil. Both view themselves as good.

They say the road to hell is paved in good intentions. By trying to make the world a better place and a "good" place, we have created "evil."

Religious people who preach against "evil" end up creating evil by bombing abortion clinics, attacking or killing people they believe are evil, starting wars, etc.

Ultimately, you can't do good without doing evil. Therefore, those who fight and crusade against evil only strengthen it.

If we want to rid the world of the bad, we must rid the world of the good as well. We must illuminate both distinctions. We can't separate them. One exists because of the other. All exist in the mind.

"when people see some things as beautiful,
other things become ugly
when people see some things as good,
other things become bad

being and non-being create each other
difficult and easy support each other
long and short define each other
high and low depend on each other
before and after follow each other"
-Tao Te Ching

Opposites cannot exist alone. Therefore, when we fight to rid ourselves of one, we suffer because it cannot be done. It's like trying to eliminate all things up so that we can always have down. It can't be done and all it would do is leave you struggling, frustrated, and angry.

We can't cease suffering in order to obtain happiness. Happiness includes the acceptance of suffering. To resist suffering is to feed suffering. What you resist persists. To fight evil is to become evil.

We cannot separate black and white, inside and outside, up and down. If we had black all the time, we wouldn't know white and therefore we wouldn't know black either. We only see the black because of the white.

If we had inside, there would have to be an outside. If we have up, there has to be a down. Neither can exist without the other.

Another problem with separating things is that we forget that things are intertwined and when one is affected, so is the other.

If we continue to separate everything within nature, we will fail to see that when we alter one aspect of nature, we dramatically alter other aspects of nature as well.

For example, let's say you had three wishes and you decided that for one of your wishes you were going to rid the world of bees.

Without bees, we would not have many plants that require bee pollination. This would affect medicines (since most contain plant extracts), clothes (no more cotton), animals that eat plants would have no food, animals that eat other animals would not have enough animals to eat and of course, we would not have enough food to eat as well. All of Earth's ecosystem would be thrown off course if all the bees in the world disappeared.

Anytime one aspect of nature is altered for our convenience, everything else is affected. All things in nature are intertwined. We cannot alter one thing without affecting everything else. Nothing in nature is separate.

We separate races, land, beliefs, sexes, and anything else that contains a different feature of something.

We've been so busy dividing, categorizing and judging that we have isolated ourselves from the social world and the natural world. We have made ourselves anxious, alone and struggling.

There are no races, only people. We are all a part of the same human race.

We must first reconcile races, then all aspects of nature and ultimately everything else. All things contain all things.

QUOTE:
"I know that my unity with all people cannot be destroyed by national boundaries and government orders." -Leo Tolstoy

---

WRITERS OF LIFE:
"True awakening will not fit into the world as you imagine it or the self you imagine yourself to be." -Adyashanti, *The End of Your World: Uncensored Straight Talk on the Nature of Enlightenment,* 2009

Everything is a story and we are all writers of life. From our childhood to our future, we create stories and meanings in everything.

We are always dreaming, creating and shaping our stories. With the help of our filter, we strengthen our beliefs and mold our stories.

When something new happens to us, we filter some information out and accept other information based on how they align with the story we want to create.

Even if you think you're not the "creative type," you are creating all the time. Every time you breathe, move or open your mouth, you are creating.

Today, you created a story out of an event. Today, you created your version of how tomorrow will look.

We are the ones who decide the story of our lives. Is your story a sad one? If it is, know that you chose it to be a sad one. Many people go through hardships, but they don't allow their lives to be defined by it. They may choose to see their story as one of survival and triumph over hardship.

Our story is what we use to define ourselves. We see ourselves as characters in a story and we act out our roles without even realizing it.

If my story is about a mother who gives her whole life and being to raising her children, then everything in my life will coordinate with my story. If something comes along that contradicts it, I reject it.

We all play roles in our lives. Roles that come with rules we didn't choose. Some people believe a mother should not work and should stay at home and be a full time mother. That is a role.

You contain multitudes. You are full of many capabilities, ideas, feelings and thoughts that go beyond being a mother. If you take on the role and exclude everything else, you deny yourself the opportunity to express yourself as you are and grow.

Some people take on more than one role. They switch from one to the other depending on where they are or who they're with.

We get trapped in roles, acting out the dramas of our stories and then we can't understand why everything feels the same or why we feel trapped or unhappy.

You write your story. You choose your theme, you choose the characters and you choose the ending.

You may not be able to choose how you die, but that is not what I mean by ending. In the end, whenever and however that may be, how did you live your life?

Were you afraid to live? Were you afraid to love? Do you regret how you have chosen to live your life?

But it's not the end and there's no point in thinking about these things. Right now, we have to realize that we have right now. That we write right now.

Past and present are illusions. Even if you feel like you've been doing the same thing, you really haven't. This is the only time you've done whatever you're doing now, and it always will be the only time. When you do something similar in a few hours, it will still not be the same thing.

You cannot step in the same river twice. Once you step in it, the river has changed; you have changed. Therefore, when you step in it, it is a different person stepping into a different river.

You are always a different person. You can never go back to being your old self.

The person who read the last paragraph is a different person than the one who is reading this one. Why? Because you have read the paragraph.

Now you are a different person again because you have just thought thoughts and felt things that you hadn't before. Since you can't erase an experience, you are now different.

Anyone you come across will be influenced and changed by you. You too will be influenced and changed by them.

As C.S. Lewis said it, "The very man who has argued you down, will sometimes be found, years later, to have been influenced by what you said."

You can't stop change, it is always happening. You are always growing and creating.

The truth is, if we don't keep ourselves present and realize that with each day we are creating, we will never get to living. We'll wake up years later and wonder what happened and how did all of those years pass so fast.

The source of most of our frustrations and anxiety are the result of living in the future or the past.

Even the most basic beliefs about reality are not true in themselves. Our thinking makes them true in our experience.

Your roles won't feel fake to you. In fact, they feel very real. Some of them give us a sense of purpose in our lives. The only negative about them is that they can hinder growth and they trap us in our roles making us feel unhappy and stuck.

So what is your story and why did you choose it? Know that you can break free from any role you have chosen. You can free yourself of unknown obligations to roles you don't remember agreeing to or creating.

It starts with awareness. When we become aware of distinctions we have created and unknowingly agreed to, we can free ourselves from them and become who we are. When we forget what we should be, we become who we are.

QUOTE:
"There is not one big cosmic meaning for all, there is only the meaning we each give to our life, an individual meaning, an individual plot, like an individual novel, a book for each person." -Anais Nin

---

MEANING AND PURPOSE:
"The privilege of a lifetime is being who you are."
-Joseph Campbell

I'm not an authority on life or any of these subjects. In fact, everything I have written about can be argued against. Your views on life and human behavior may be just as valid or invalid as mine. Both can be argued and both can be criticized. It's not a matter for argument. It's a matter of what makes your life whole, complete, and peaceful. What makes you happy?

If your current state of mind is one you intentionally choose to keep, you are not wrong for it. That's really the point I want to make. There is no wrong and right when it comes to how we choose to live our lives. There is only what works and what doesn't work.

If you repeat the same act repeatedly expecting different results, you will soon see that it's not working. You may then choose to change the act to something that does work.

The same act, however, might work for someone else. It's not about everyone else and what works for them. It's about what works for you. This book is for you.

Life is what you make of it. Most everything in it exists in the mind: happiness, suffering, love, hate, separation, what we see, how we see it, what we experience and how we experience it. Life is an internal state, not a physical act. The world outside exists inside.

If your current state of mind (beliefs, behaviors, thoughts and feelings) cause you misery and pain, why choose to continue with them?

Your misery will not make you healthier, happier or more peaceful. It will not benefit your family, friends or others.

We all have to figure out our own way. One person's right can be another's wrong, therefore, we can't have permanent right and wrong, only perspective.

"Meaning"

If you were on an airplane, everything would look small to you. If you were standing on the ground, underneath skyscrapers, everything would look big to you.

To you, you are an individual being. From the perspective of a single cell in your body, you are a collection of fifty million cells, several organs, tissues and muscles. To a cell, you are a community. You are not an individual being. You are many beings housed in one body. Just like humans are many beings housed on Earth.

Everything in life is dependent on perspective. Therefore, we must not judge others harshly on what they choose to believe or why they choose to believe it. Most of the time, they don't even know or understand the reason why they do. Most of it is taught from childhood and subconscious.

It is not our place to judge. Our responsibility is to figure out our purpose in life, not judge others in their purpose.

Your purpose may be very different from mine. Is your purpose right and my purpose wrong?

The nose can't replace the eyes and the mouth can't replace the ears. The liver can't replace the heart and the intestines can't replace the brain. Everything has its own identity and purpose that can't be substituted by another thing.

The organs are separate but connected, just as we all are. We may have different shapes, colors, beliefs and functions but we are all connected.

Can the tree replace the river? Can the mountain replace the sun?

Can the sun make the tree wrong for giving oxygen? Can the tree make the sun wrong for giving warmth?

The river flows, the mountain stands motionless. A river can't stand motionless or else it's not a river. The mountain can't flow or else it's not a mountain. Is one right and the other wrong?

They each serve their purpose. They don't compete against each other, they don't judge each other and they don't make each other wrong.

Can I make you wrong for being a taxi driver, garbage collector or teacher? Can you make me wrong for being a writer? Moreover, what would be the point? What purpose would it serve if we all went around making each other wrong? We can't all be doctors. Who would fly the planes, bake the bread, build houses, teach the youth, drive the buses, collect the trash, wire the electricity and fix the pipes?

Each being finds that which is right for them. There isn't one way to live. One is no more right in how it's being than the other.

We all contribute in our own way. No one is wrong for whatever it is they contribute. We add to the lives we connect with everyday and that sends ripples down to the people they connect with and the people they connect with.

Like the little ripples in water that begin in a small area and widen as it spreads across the ocean, we too leave ripples everywhere we go and with every life we come in contact with.

The classic American movie, "It's a Wonderful Life" makes this point exactly. It follows the life of George Bailey, who always wanted to travel and see the world. However, every time he had the opportunity to leave his small town and travel, there was some family emergency that caused him to stay.

Later in the movie, his father dies and his brother goes off to war and he is left having to stay and take care of his father's banking business. He marries, has kids and settles in town.

Then one day, the bank's money is lost. He is forced to tell the people in town that their money is gone and close the bank.

He decides that it would be best if he killed himself. As he is about to throw himself off the bridge, an angel appears and shows him what life would be like for everyone else if he had never lived.

He goes through the rest of the movie seeing what his friends, family, neighborhood and town would be like if he had never been born. All of those people he had helped were left without his help. Even though it was the same people and the same town, everything and everyone was different because they had never known him.

In the end, he discovers that he had a wonderful life, not because he had a house or a business but because his life had caused a great ripple effect in so many other lives. He found value in his life because of how he had affected others.

None of us really realizes the affect we have on others. We are far more powerful than we imagine. One person's life changes the world, whether we realize it or not.

One day at my old work in the Juvenile Probation Department, a health inspector came by the office to teach us about safety. In between her sessions, she sat with us in the clerk's room and we chatted about life.

She asked me about my major in college and I told her that I was a philosophy major. She asked me if I had ever heard of Alan Watts and then she suggested that I read his book, "Wisdom of Insecurity."

That suggestion changed my life and eventually lead me to write this book. Reading one book that she recommended lead to another and another and soon my filter, thoughts, beliefs and feelings had completely changed.

My world changed because of a woman whose name I don't even remember. She probably doesn't remember her suggestion, our conversation or me. I don't know if she will ever realize what she did for me.

Something as simple as recommending a book or a smile in passing can go a very long way.

We've become conditioned to quick gratification; if we don't see the immediate consequences, reactions or benefits to our actions, we assume it's not there. Just because you didn't see the ripple effect of your actions doesn't mean you didn't have an impact. You may have planted a seed within them that will someday grow and generate fruit.

There's a saying, "If you know six people, you know the world." Those six people know six people and so on. The world is within your home, your neighborhood, your workplace, your classroom, etc. There is no need to search the world to find happiness, to find yourself or to find life.

You are who you choose to be. Just know whom it is you choose to be. Many times, we become what we think others want us to become and we forget we chose to be that.

To be yourself in a world that is constantly trying to make you someone else is the ultimate accomplishment. They can criticize you, blame you and hate you, but their blame and criticism can't injure you and their praise can't elevate you. You are who you are and nothing anyone says, whether it be positive or negative, can change that.

QUOTE:
"To know that even one life has breathed easier because you have lived, this is to have succeeded."
-Ralph Waldo Emerson

YOU:
"Today you are You, that is truer than true. There is no one alive who is Youer than You." -Dr. Seuss

Who are you? Are you the role you play? Are you what you have, own and possess? Are you your gender, sex or marital status? Who are you? What does that mean?

In the trillions of people who have ever been born, and the billions that exist now, there is only one you. You are unique.

Even if we cloned you, it might look like you and carry your same DNA but because of the different upbringing, memories and environmental factors, it would be a different person.

Why do we then view ourselves as just like everyone else? Why do we work to become like everyone else? Moreover, who is this one person we are all trying to be like? Did this person try to be like someone else and did that someone else try to be like another person?

When you realize that you are aware, unique and connected to all things, you will see how powerful you truly are in your life. Others may have useful perspectives and good intentions but ultimately, it is your choices that hold any value in creating your destiny.

Just by reading this book, your filter has changed. You have changed. It doesn't matter if you agree with any of the ideas presented in it. Since the ideas have been brought to your attention, your mind will attempt to test these theories whether you realize it or not. You will now begin to see the things mentioned in this book all around you.

Please feel free to test them. If they work for you, if they improve your life, keep them. If they don't, let them go. That's my general philosophy in life.

I review my thoughts, beliefs, behaviors and habits and ask the question, does it help or hurt me? Is it going to improve my life and being or cause me pain? Does this way of thinking benefit my wellbeing or cause suffering?

One of the most important things to keep in mind is that beliefs change, they are neither permanent nor absolute truths. They are relative truths reinforced by our experiences.

Regardless of our experiences, there is an innate goodness and compassion within all of us. Some time ago, in the chaos of life, we lost ourselves. We lost ourselves in the frantic race we run every day.

We run toward security, trapping ourselves in jobs, marriages and situations that make us miserable.

We run toward material objects we believe will make us happy; buying, collecting and accumulating things we believe hold value and then we live in fear of losing them.

We run away from each other trying to prove our independence, we hurt each other to fill up our egos and we put each other down to hide our own pain.

We destroy our health chasing after money, feel anxious over losing our money and then we become sick and use up all that money to fix our health.

We run this crazy race we call life; exhausting ourselves, feeling tired, miserable and empty. We run not because that is how life is experienced, but because we witnessed others running and decided to join the race.

"Meaning"

We work so hard most of our lives trying to change ourselves. Trying to "improve" unique characteristics of ourselves that don't fit into other people's ideas of who we should be. You require no improvement.

We fight ourselves. We fight others. We fight life.

When you forget what you "should" be, you become what you are. When you know who you are, other people's praise can't elevate you and their criticism can't hurt you.

There is no need to fight, to run or to change. In fact, if you see yourself correctly, you would see that you are perfect as you are and don't require improvements.

That may seem contradictory to most of the things discussed in this book, but it's not contradictory at all.

You don't need to change who you are. You just need to discover who you are. Your only responsibility is to be yourself instead of fighting and working to become predefined versions of yourself.

Your mind may search for examples of behaviors or characteristics of people that might require change; alcoholism, anger, drug abuse, etc.

Ultimately, that's what this book is for. If you can see which thoughts, feelings, behaviors and misinterpretations are leading to destructive escapism, then the doors are open for you to be you. The you who is not an alcoholic, angry or abusive.

If you really see yourself correctly, you wouldn't feel the need to drink. If we saw ourselves for what we truly are, we wouldn't feel the need to become violent, do drugs or engage in any other self-destructive activity.

If we saw others and ourselves from a different perspective, we wouldn't feel inferior to others and therefore feel the need to treat people appallingly to make ourselves feel better. We wouldn't feel the need to destroy ourselves or others if we saw ourselves for what we are.

All human ills are a result of misconception. Sadness, anger and suffering are a result of our misperception of others and ourselves.

You are perfect as you are. There is no need to make yourself sick with stress, worry, food, alcohol, drugs, gambling, smoking or any other tool we use to numb our unnecessary suffering.

All that is required of us is to be what we were created to be: ourselves. You were created to be you. You were not created to be me; you were not created to be Jesus, Buddha, Muhammad, your parents or anyone else. You cannot replace anyone and no one can replace you.

It is your job to be you. First, however, you must figure out who that is. Beneath the layers of societal and parental beliefs, prejudices and habits lies an exceptional entity that is a part of everything and can't be replaced by anything.

I'm providing for you a tool to help you discover yourself outside of false beliefs, automatic reactions, self-defeating habits, negative conditioning and the chaos of your mind.

When all of that is stripped away, what is left? You. The real you. Whoever that may be. Perhaps one day the both of us will be privileged enough to meet whoever that happens to be.

QUOTE:

"Your vision will become clear only when you look into your heart. Whoever looks outside, dreams. Who looks inside, awakens." -Carl Jung

"What I am really saying is that you don't need to do anything, because if you see yourself in the correct way, you are all as much extraordinary phenomenon of nature as tress, clouds, the patterns in running water, the flickering of fire, the arrangement of the stars, and the form of a galaxy. You are all just like that, and there is nothing wrong with you at all."

-Alan Watts, *Still the Mind*

About the Author:

Emily Maroutian was born in Yerevan Armenia in August of 1984. She moved to the United States at the age of five. She currently resides in Los Angeles, California.

She created Maroutian Entertainment in early 2009. She also writes books, screenplays, short stories and poems.

19356143R00143

Made in the USA
San Bernardino, CA
22 February 2015